Poems of Fun and Fancy

Barnes & Noble Poetry Library

CHRISTMAS POEMS

LOVE POEMS

POEMS OF FUN AND FANCY

POEMS OF THE AMERICAN SPIRIT

POEMS OF VISION AND PROPHECY

POEMS OF FUN AND FANCY

SERIES EDITOR
DAVID STANFORD BURR

BARNES & NOBLE POETRY LIBRARY

The acknowledgments appearing on page 239
constitute an extension of this copyright page.

2002 Barnes & Noble Books

ISBN 0-7607-3313-9

Text design by Rhea Braunstein

Printed and bound in the United States of America

02 03 04 05 M 9 8 7 6 5 4 3 2

RRD-C

Contents

Foreword

Poems of Fun and Fancy explores the full range of playful, imaginative poetry, including ersatz Latin, gobbledygook, limericks, clerihews, alphabet poems, menu poems, riddles, scientific proofs, paradoxes, light-opera parodies, and humorous imitations of famous poets. Many of these poems concern animals: both the common—or uncommon, if we consider "whether pigs have wings"—found on a farm and the marvelous beasts such as Lewis Carroll's Jabberwocky or Ogden Nash's Wendigo or Edward Lear's Dong with its luminous nose. These three poets' names are well known for their nonsense verse, and they are joined by scores of other famous practitioners, including William Shakespeare, François Rabelais, Stevie Smith, W. S. Gilbert, E. E. Cummings, Wallace Stevens, Jonathan Swift, A. E. Housman, Shel Silverstein, Eugene Field, and many others. Some of the selections in this collection are five hundred years old, but all retain their freshness and spirit of fun.

Read these poems out loud and let their cadences take you into a wonderland that often seems almost real and rational. They will confound, astound, and hold you spellbound, beguiling you with their wit, imagination, and poetic fun and fancy.

—DAVID STANFORD BURR

Poems of Fun and Fancy

"Hey, diddle, diddle!"

Hey, diddle, diddle!
The cat and the fiddle,
The cow jumped over the moon;
The little dog laughed
To see such sport,
And the dish ran away with the spoon.

MOTHER GOOSE (18TH CENTURY)

"If all the seas were one sea,"

If all the seas were one sea,
What a *great* sea that would be!
If all the trees were one tree,
What a *great* tree that would be!
If all the axes were one ax,
What a *great* ax that would be!
If all the men were one man,
What a *great* man he would be!
And if the *great* man took the *great* ax,
And cut down the *great* tree,
And let it fall into the *great* sea,
What a *great* splash-splash that would be!

MOTHER GOOSE (18TH CENTURY)

"There were three jovial huntsmen,"

There were three jovial huntsmen,
As I have heard them say,
And they would go a-hunting
All on a summer's day.

All the day they hunted,
And nothing could they find
But a ship a-sailing,
A-sailing with the wind.

One said it was a ship.
The other he said nay;
The third said it was a house
With the chimney blown away.

And all the night they hunted,
And nothing could they find
But the moon a-gliding,
A-gliding with the wind.

One said it was the moon,
The other he said nay;
The third said it was a cheese,
And half o't cut away.

Old Mother Hubbard

Old Mother Hubbard
Went to the cupboard,
To give her poor dog a bone;
But when she got there
The cupboard was bare,
And so the poor dog had none.

She went to the baker's
To buy him some bread;
When she came back
The dog was dead.

She went to the undertaker's
To buy him a coffin;
When she got back
The dog was laughing.

She took a clean dish
To get him some tripe;
When she came back
He was smoking a pipe.

She went to the alehouse
To get him some beer;
When she came back
The dog sat in a chair.

She went to the tavern
For white wine and red;
When she came back
The dog stood on his head.

She went to the hatter's
To buy him a hat;
When she came back
He was feeding the cat.

She went to the barber's
To buy him a wig;
When she came back
He was dancing a jig.

She went to the fruiterer's
To buy him some fruit;
When she came back
He was playing the flute.

She went to the tailor's
To buy him a coat;
When she came back
He was riding a goat.

She went to the cobbler's
To buy him some shoes;

stanza continues

When she came back
  He was reading the news.

She went to the sempster's
  To buy him some linen;
When she came back
  The dog was a-spinning.

She went to the hosier's
  To buy him some hose;
When she came back
  He was dressed in his clothes.

The dame made a curtsy,
  The dog made a bow;
The dame said, "Your servant,"
  The dog said, "Bow-wow."

The Little Star

Scintillate, scintillate, globule orific,
Fain would I fathom thy nature's specific.
Loftily poised in ether capacious,
Strongly resembling a gem carbonaceous.

When torrid Phoebus refuses his presence
And ceases to lamp with fierce incandescence,
Then you illumine the regions supernal,
Scintillate, scintillate, semper nocturnal.

Then the victim of hospiceless peregrination
Gratefully hails your minute coruscation.
He could not determine his journey's direction
But for your bright scintillating protection.

ANONYMOUS

The Star

Twinkle, twinkle, little star,
How I wonder what you are!
Up above the world so high,
Like a diamond in the sky.

When the blazing sun is gone,
When he nothing shines upon,
Then you show your little light,
Twinkle, twinkle, all the night.

Then the traveller in the dark,
Thanks you for your tiny spark!
He could not see which way to go,
If you did not twinkle so.

In the dark blue sky you keep,
And often through my curtains peep,
For you never shut your eye
Till the sun is in the sky.

As your bright and tiny spark
Lights the traveller in the dark,
Though I know not what you are,
Twinkle, twinkle, little star.

ANN & JANE TAYLOR (19TH CENTURY)

An Elegy on the Death of a Mad Dog

Good people all, of every sort,
  Give ear unto my song;
And if you find it wondrous short, —
  It cannot hold you long.

In Islington there was a man,
  Of whom the world might say
That still a godly race he ran, —
  Whene'er he went to pray.

A kind and gentle heart he had,
  To comfort friends and foes;
The naked every day he clad, —
  When he put on his clothes.

And in that town a dog was found,
  As many dogs there be,
Both mongrel, puppy, whelp, and hound,
  And curs of low degree.

The dog and man at first were friends;
  But when a pique began,
The dog, to gain some private ends,
  Went mad, and bit the man.

continues

OLIVER GOLDSMITH (1728–1774)

Around from all the neighboring streets,
The wondering neighbors ran,
And swore the dog had lost his wits
To bite so good a man.

The wound it seemed both sore and sad
To every Christian eye;
And while they swore the dog was mad
They swore the man would die.

But soon a wonder came to light,
That showed the rogues they lied;
The man recovered of the bite,
The dog it was that died.

Nonsense

Like to the thund'ring tone of unspoke speeches,
Or like a lobster clad in logic breeches,
Or like the gray frieze of a crimson cat,
Or like a moon-calf in a slipshoo hat,
Or like a shadow when the sun is gone,
Or like a thought that ne'er was thought upon,
  Even such is man, who never was begotten
  Until his children were both dead and rotten.

Like to the fiery touchstone of a cabbage,
Or like a crablouse with his bag and baggage,
Or like th'abortive issue of a fizzle,
Or like the bag-pudding of a plowman's whistle,
Or like the four-square circle of a ring,
Or like the singing of hey down a ding,
  Even such is man, who, breathless without doubt,
  Spake to small purpose when his tongue was out.

Like to the green fresh fading withered rose,
Or like to rhyme or verse that runs in prose,
Or like the humbles of a tinder-box,
Or like a man that's sound, yet hath the pox,
Or like a hobnail coin'd in single pence,
Or like the present preterperfect tense,
  Even such is man, who died and then did laugh
  To see such strange lines writ on's epitaph.

RICHARD CORBETT (1582–1635)

"Three Nonsense Poems"

I saw Esau sawing wood,
And Esau saw I saw him;
Though Esau saw I saw him saw,
Still Esau went on sawing.

Eaper weaper, chimbley-sweeper,
Had a wife but couldn't keep her,
Had anovver, didn't love her,
Up the chimbley he did shove her.

There was a man of Thessaly,
  And he was wondrous wise,
He jumped into a bramble bush
  And scratched out both his eyes.
And when he saw his eyes were out,
  With all his might and main
He jumped into another bush
  And scratched them in again.

The Dong with a Luminous Nose

When awful darkness and silence reign
Over the great Gromboolian plain,
  Through the long, long wintry nights;—
When the angry breakers roar
As they beat on the rocky shore;—
  When Storm-clouds brood on the towering heights
Of the Hills of the Chankly Bore:—
Then, through the vast and gloomy dark,
There moves what seems a fiery spark,
  A lonely spark with silvery rays
  Piercing the coal-black night,—
  A Meteor strange and bright:—
Hither and thither the vision strays,
  A single lurid light.

Slowly it wanders,—pauses,—creeps,—
Anon it sparkles,—flashes and leaps;
And ever as onward it gleaming goes
A light on the Bong-tree stems it throws.
And those who watch at that midnight hour
From Hall or Terrace, or lofty Tower,
Cry, as the wild light passes along,—
    'The Dong!—the Dong!

stanza continues

The wandering Dong through the forest goes!
The Dong! the Dong!
The Dong with a luminous Nose!'

Long years ago
The Dong was happy and gay,
Till he fell in love with a Jumbly Girl
Who came to those shores one day,
For the Jumblies came in a sieve, they did,—
Landing at eve near the Zemmery Fidd
Where the Oblong Oysters grow,
And the rocks are smooth and gray.
And all the woods and the valleys rang
With the Chorus they daily and nightly sang,—
'Far and few, far and few,
Are the lands where the Jumblies live;
Their heads are green, and their hands are blue
And they went to sea in a sieve.'

Happily, happily passed those days!
While the cheerful Jumblies staid;
They danced in circlets all night long,
To the plaintive pipe of the lively Dong,
In moonlight, shine, or shade.
For day and night he was always there
By the side of the Jumbly Girl so fair,

stanza continues

With her sky-blue hands, and her sea-green hair.
Till the morning came of that hateful day
When the Jumblies sailed in their sieve away,
And the Dong was left on the cruel shore
Gazing—gazing for evermore,—
Ever keeping his weary eyes on
That pea-green sail on the far horizon,—
Singing the Jumbly Chorus still
As he sate all day on the grassy hill,—
'Far and few, far and few,
Are the lands where the Jumblies live;
Their heads are green, and their hands are blue,
And they went to sea in a sieve.'

But when the sun was low in the West,
The Dong arose and said;—
—'What little sense I once possessed
Has quite gone out of my head!'—
And since that day he wanders still
By lake and forest, marsh and hill,
Singing—'O somewhere, in valley or plain
Might I find my Jumbly Girl again!
For ever I'll seek by lake and shore
Till I find my Jumbly Girl once more!'

continues

Playing a pipe with silvery squeaks,
Since then his Jumbly Girl he seeks,
And because by night he could not see,
He gathered the bark of the Twangum Tree
On the flowery plain that grows.
And he wove him a wondrous Nose,—
A Nose as strange as a Nose could be!
Of vast proportions and painted red,
And tied with cords to the back of his head.
—In a hollow rounded space it ended
With a luminous Lamp within suspended,
All fenced about
With a bandage stout
To prevent the wind from blowing it out;—
And with holes all round to send the light,
In gleaming rays on the dismal night.

And now each night, and all night long,
Over those plains still roams the Dong;
And above the wail of the Chimp and Snipe
You may hear the squeak of his plaintive pipe
While ever he seeks, but seeks in vain
To meet with his Jumbly Girl again;
Lonely and wild—all night he goes,—
The Dong with a luminous Nose!
And all who watch at the midnight hour,
From Hall or Terrace, or lofty Tower,

stanza continues

Cry, as they trace the Meteor bright,
Moving along through the dreary night,—
  'This is the hour when forth he goes,
  The Dong with a luminous Nose!
  Yonder—over the plain he goes;
    He goes!
    He goes;
  The Dong with a luminous Nose!'

The Wendigo

The Wendigo,
The Wendigo!
Its eyes are ice and indigo!
Its blood is rank and yellowish!
Its voice is hoarse and bellowish!
Its tentacles are slithery,
And scummy,
Slimy,
Leathery!
Its lips are hungry blubbery,
And smacky,
Sucky,
Rubbery!
The Wendigo,
The Wendigo!
I saw it just a friend ago!
Last night it lurked in Canada;
Tonight, on your veranada!
As you are lolling hammockwise
It contemplates you stomachwise.
You loll,
It contemplates,
It lollops.
The rest is merely gulps and gollops.

OGDEN NASH (1902–1971)

Jabberwocky

'Twas brillig, and the slithy toves
  Did gyre and gimble in the wabe;
All mimsy were the borogoves,
    And the mome raths outgrabe.

'Beware the Jabberwock, my son!
  The jaws that bite, the claws that catch!
Beware the Jubjub bird, and shun
    The frumious Bandersnatch!'

He took his vorpal sword in hand:
  Long time the manxome foe he sought—
So rested he by the Tumtum tree,
    And stood awhile in thought.

And as in uffish thought he stood,
  The Jabberwock, with eyes of flame,
Came whiffling through the tulgey wood,
    And burbled as it came!

One, two! One, two! And through and through
  The vorpal blade went snicker-snack!
He left it dead, and with its head
    He went galumphing back.

continues

'And hast thou slain the Jabbberwock?
  Come to my arms, my beamish boy!
O frabjous day! Callooh! Callay!'
    He chortled in his joy.

'Twas brillig, and the slithy toves
  Did gyre and gimble in the wabe;
All mimsy were the borogoves,
    And the mome raths outgrabe.

Sir Eglamour

Sir Eglamour, that worthy knight,
He took his sword and went to fight;
And as he rode both hill and dale,
Armëd upon his shirt of mail,
A dragon came out of his den,
Had slain, God knows how many men!

When he espied Sir Eglamour,
Oh, if you had but heard him roar,
And seen how all the trees did shake,
The knight did tremble, horse did quake,
The birds betake them all to peeping—
It would have made you fall a weeping!

But now it is vain to fear,
Being come unto, 'fight dog! fight bear!'
To it they go and fiercely fight
A live-long day from morn till night.
The dragon had a plaguy hide,
And could the sharpest steel abide.

No sword will enter him with cuts,
Which vexed the knight unto the guts;

stanza continues

SAMUEL ROWLANDS (1570?–1630?)

But, as in choler he did burn,
He watched the dragon a good turn;
And, as a yawning he did fall,
He thrust his sword in, hilts and all.

Then, like a coward, he did fly
Unto his den that was hard by;
And there he lay all night and roared.
The knight was sorry for his sword,
But, riding thence, said, 'I forsake it,
He that will fetch it, let him take it!'

The Carelesse Nurse Mayd

I sawe a Mayd sitte on a Bank,
Beguiled by Wooer fayne and fond;
And whiles His flatterynge Vowes She drank,
Her Nurselynge slipt within a Pond!

All Even Tide they Talkde and Kist,
For She was fayre and He was Kinde;
The Sunne went down before She wist
Another Sonne had sett behinde!

With angrie Hands and frownynge Browe,
That deemed Her owne the Urchine's Sinne,
She pluckt Him out, but he was nowe
Past being Whipt for fallynge in.

She then beginnes to wayle the Ladde
With Shrikes that Echo answerde round—
O! foolishe Mayd to be soe sadde
The Momente that her Care was drownd!

THOMAS HOOD (1799–1845)

"Sigh no more, ladies, sigh no more,"

from *MUCH ADO ABOUT NOTHING*

Sigh no more, ladies, sigh no more,
  Men were deceivers ever;
One foot in sea, and one on shore;
  To one thing constant never:
      Then sigh not so,
      But let them go,
  And be you blithe and bonny;
Converting all your sounds of woe
  Into Hey nonny, nonny.

Sing no more ditties, sing no more
  Of dumps so dull and heavy;
The fraud of men were ever so,
  Since summer first was leavy.
      Then sigh not so,
      But let them go,
  And be you blithe and bonny;
Converting all your sounds of woe
  Into Hey nonny, nonny.

The Elderly Gentleman

By the side of a murmuring stream an elderly
gentleman sat.
On the top of his head was a wig, and a-top of his
wig was his hat.

The wind it blew high and blew strong, as the
elderly gentleman sat;
And bore from his head in a trice, and plunged in
the river his hat.

The gentleman then took his cane which lay by his
side as he sat;
And he dropped in the river his wig, in attempting
to get out his hat.

His breast it grew cold with despair, and full in his
eye madness sat;
So he flung in the river his cane to swim with his
wig, and his hat.

Cool reflection at last came across while this elderly
gentleman sat;
So he thought he would follow the stream and look
for his cane, wig, and hat.

continues

GEORGE CANNING (1770–1827)

His head being thicker than common, o'er-balanced
the rest of his fat;
And in plumped this son of a woman to follow his
wig, cane, and hat.

Malum Opus

Prope ripam fluvii solus
  A senex silently sat;
Super capitum ecce his wig,
  Et wig super, ecce his hat.

Blew Zephyrus alte, acerbus,
  Dum elderly gentleman sat;
Et a capite took up quite torve
  Et in rivum projecit his hat.

Tunc soft maledixit the old man,
  Tunc stooped from the bank where he sat
Et cum scipio poked in the water,
  Conatus servare his hat.

Blew Zephyrus alte, acerbus,
  The moment it saw him at that;
Et whisked his novum scratch wig
  In flumen, along with his hat.

Ab imo pectore damnavit
  In cœruleus eye dolor sat;
Tunc despairingly threw in his cane
  Nare cum his wig and his hat.

continues

L'Envoi

Contra bonos mores, don't swear
  It 'est wicked you know (verbum sat),
Si this tale habet no other moral
  Mehercle! You 're gratus to that!

Intramural Aestivation, or Summer in Town, by a Teacher of Latin

In candent ire the solar splendor flames;
The foles, languescent, pend from arid rames;
His humid front the cive, anheling, wipes,
And dreams of erring on ventiferous ripes.

How dulce to vive occult to mortal eyes,
Dorm on the herb with none to supervise,
Carp the suave berries from the crescent vine,
And bibe the flow from longicaudate kine!

To me, alas! no verdurous visions come,
Save yon exiguous pool's conferva-scum,—
No concave vast repeats the tender hue
That laves my milk-jug with celestial blue!

Me wretched! Let me curr to quercine shades!
Effund your albid hausts, lactiferous maids!
O, might I vole to some umbrageous clump,—
Depart,—be off,—excede,—evade,—erump!

Tenuous and Precarious

Tenuous and Precarious
Were my guardians,
Precarious and Tenuous,
Two Romans.

My father was Hazardous,
Hazardous,
Dear old man,
Three Romans.

There was my brother Spurious,
Spurious Posthumous,
Spurious was spurious
Was four Romans.

My husband was Perfidious,
He was perfidious,
Five Romans.

Surreptitious, our son,
Was surreptitious,
He was six Romans.

Our cat Tedious
Still lives,
Count not Tedious
Yet.

My name is Finis,
Finis, Finis,
I am Finis,
Six, five, four, three, two,
One Roman,
Finis.

STEVIE SMITH (1903–1971)

Alphabet

A tumbled down, and hurt his Arm, against a bit of wood.
B said, 'My Boy, O! do not cry; it cannot do you good!'
C said, 'A Cup of Coffee hot can't do you any harm.'
D said, 'A Doctor should be fetched, and he would cure the arm.'
E said, 'An Egg beat up with milk would quickly make him well.'
F said, 'A Fish, if broiled, might cure, if only by the smell.'
G said, 'Green Gooseberry fool, the best of cures I hold.'
H said, 'His Hat should be kept on, to keep him from the cold.'
I said, 'Some Ice upon his head will make him better soon.'
J said, 'Some Jam, if spread on bread, or given in a spoon!'
K said, 'A Kangaroo is here,—this picture let him see.'
L said, 'A Lamp pray keep alight, to make some barley tea.'
M said, 'A Mulberry or two might give him satisfaction.'

EDWARD LEAR (1812–1888)

N said, 'Some Nuts, if rolled about, might be a slight attraction.'
O said, 'An Owl might make him laugh, if only it would wink.'
P said, 'Some Poetry might be read aloud, to make him think.'
Q said, 'A Quince I recommend, — a Quince, or else a Quail.'
R said, 'Some Rats might make him move, if fastened by their tail.'
S said, 'A Song should now be sung, in hopes to make him laugh!'
T said, 'A Turnip might avail, if sliced or cut in half!'
U said, 'An Urn, with water hot, place underneath his chin!'
V said, 'I'll stand upon a chair, and play a Violin!'
W said, 'Some Whisky-Whizzgigs fetch, some marbles and a ball!'
X said, 'Some double XX ale would be the best of all!'
Y said, 'Some Yeast mixed up with salt would make a perfect plaster!'
Z said, 'Here is a box of Zinc! Get in, my little master!

We'll shut you up! We'll nail you down!
We will, my little master!
We think we've all heard quite enough of this your sad disaster!'

To Minerva

My temples throb, my pulses boil,
  I'm sick of Song and Ode, and Ballad—
So, Thyrsis, take the Midnight Oil
  And pour it on a lobster salad.

My brain is dull, my sight is foul,
  I cannot write a verse, or read—
Then, Pallas, take away thine Owl,
  And let us have a lark instead.

THOMAS HOOD (1799–1845)

Namby-Pamby

A Panegyric on the New Versification
Address'd to A---P---, Esq.

Naughty Paughty Jack-a-Dandy,
Stole a Piece of Sugar Candy
From the Grocer's Shoppy-Shop,
And away did hoppy-hop.

All ye poets of the age,
All ye witlings of the stage,
Learn your jingles to reform,
Crop your numbers to conform.
Let your little verses flow
Gently, sweetly, row by row;
Let the verse the subject fit,
Little subject, little wit.
Namby-Pamby is your guide,
Albion's joy, Hibernia's pride.
Namby-Pamby, pilly-piss,
Rhimy-pim'd on Missy Miss
Tartaretta Tartaree,
From the navel to the knee;
That her father's gracy-grace
Might give him a placey place.

continues

HENRY CAREY (1687?–1743)

He no longer writes of Mammy
Andromache and her lammy,
Hanging-panging at the breast
Of a matron most distress'd.
Now the venal poet sings
Baby clouts and baby things,
Baby dolls and baby houses,
Little misses, little spouses,
Little playthings, little toys,
Little girls and little boys.
As an actor does his part,
So the nurses get by heart
Namby-Pamby's little rhimes,
Little jingles, little chimes,
To repeat to missy-miss,
Piddling ponds of pissy-piss;
Cracking-packing like a lady,
Or bye-bying in the crady.
Namby-Pamby's doubly mild,
Once a man, and twice a child;
To his hanging sleeves restor'd,
Now he foots it like a lord;
Now he pumps his little wits,
Shitting writes, and writing shits,
All by little tiny bits.
And methinks I hear him say,
Boys and girls, come out to play!
Moon do's shine as bright as day.

Now my Namby-Pamby's found
Sitting on the friar's ground,
Picking silver, picking gold;
Namby-Pamby's never old.
Bally-cally, they begin,
Namby-Pamby still keeps in.
Namby-Pamby is no clown.
London Bridge is broken down:
Now he courts the gay ladee,
Dancing o'er the Lady-Lee.
Now he sings of Lick-spit Lyar,
Burning in the brimstone fire;
Lyar, lyar! Lick-spit, Lick,
Turn about the candle stick!
Now he sings of Jacky Horner,
Sitting in the chimney corner,
Eating of a Christmas pye,
Putting in his thumb, O fie!
Putting in, O fie! his thumb,
Pulling out, O strange, a plum.
Now he plays at Stee-Staw-Stud,
Sticking apples in the mud;
When 'tis turn'd to Stee-Staw-Stire,
Then he sticks them in the mire,
Now he acts the grenadier,
Calling for a pot of beer.

stanza continues

Where's his money? He's forgot;
Get him gone, a drunken sot.
Now a cock-horse does he ride,
And anon on timber stride.
See and Saw, and Sacch'ry Down,
London is a gallant town!
Now he gathers riches in,
Thicker, faster, pin by pin;
Pins apiece to see his show,
Boys and girls flock row by row;
From their clothes the pins they take,
Risk a whipping for his sake;
From their cloaths the pins they pull
To fill Namby's cushion full.
So much wit at such an age
Does a genius great presage;
Second childhood gone and past,
Should he prove a man at last,
What must second manhood be
In a child so bright as he.

Guard him, ye poetic pow'rs,
Watch his minutes, watch his hours;
Let your tuneful nine inspire him;
Let the poets, one and all,
To his genius victims fall.

Handy Pandy

Handy Pandy, Jack-a-dandy,
Loves plum cake and sugar candy.
He bought some at a grocer's shop,
And out he came, hop, hop, hop!

MOTHER GOOSE (18TH CENTURY)

London Bridge

London Bridge is broken down,
  Dance o'er my Lady Lee;
London bridge is broken down,
  With a gay ladye.

How shall we build it up again?
  Dance o'er my Lady Lee;
How shall we build it up again?
  With a gay ladye.

Silver and gold will be stole away,
  Dance o'er my Lady Lee;
Silver and gold will be stole away,
  With a gay ladye.

Build it up again with iron and steel,
  Dance o'er my Lady Lee;
Build it up with iron and steel,
  With a gay ladye.

Iron and steel will bend and bow,
  Dance o'er my Lady Lee;
Iron and steel will bend and bow,
  With a gay ladye.

Build it up with wood and clay,
  Dance o'er my Lady Lee;
Build it up with wood and clay,
  With a gay ladye.

Wood and clay will wash away,
  Dance o'er my Lady Lee;
Wood and clay will wash away,
  With a gay ladye.

Build it up with stone so strong,
  Dance o'er my Lady Lee;
Huzza! 'twill last for ages long,
  With a gay ladye.

"A Pair of Jacks"

JACK

Jack be nimble, Jack be quick,
Jack jump over the candlestick.

LITTLE JACK HORNER

Little Jack Horner
Sat in the corner,
  Eating a Christmas pie:
He put in his thumb,
And pulled out a plum,
  And said, "What a good boy am I!"

Poeta Fit, non Nascitur

'How shall I be a poet?
  How shall I write in rhyme:
You told me once "the very wish
  Partook of the sublime."
Then tell me how! Don't put me off
  With your "another time"!'

The old man smiled to see him,
  To hear his sudden sally;
He liked the lad to speak his mind
  Enthusiastically;
And thought 'There's no hum-drum in him,
  Nor any shilly-shally.'

'And would you be a poet
  Before you've been to school?
Ah, well! I hardly thought you
  So absolute a fool.
First learn to be spasmodic—
  A very simple rule.

'For first you write a sentence,
  And then you chop it small;
Then mix the bits, and sort them out

stanza continues

Just as they chance to fall:
The order of the phrases makes
No difference at all.

'Then, if you'd be impressive,
Remember what I say,
That abstract qualities begin
With capitals alway:
The True, the Good, the Beautiful—
Those are the things that pay!

'Next, when you are describing
A shape, or sound, or tint;
Don't state the matter plainly,
But put it in a hint;
And learn to look at all things
With a sort of mental squint.'

'For instance, if I wished, Sir,
Of mutton-pies to tell,
Should I say "dreams of fleecy flocks
Pent in a wheaten cell"?'
'Why, yes,' the old man said: 'that phrase
Would answer very well.

'Then fourthly, there are epithets
That suit with any word—

stanza continues

As well as Harvey's Reading Sauce
   With fish, or flesh, or bird—
Of these, "wild," "lonely," "weary," "strange,"
   Are much to be preferred.'

'And will it do, O will it do
   To take them in a lump—
As "the wild man went his weary way
   To a strange and lonely pump"?'
   'Nay, nay! You must not hastily
   To such conclusions jump.

'Such epithets, like pepper,
   Give zest to what you write;
And, if you strew them sparely,
   They whet the appetite:
But if you lay them on too thick,
   You spoil the matter quite!

'Last, as to the arrangement:
   Your reader, you should show him.
Must take what information he
   Can get, and look for no im-
mature disclosure of the drift
   And purpose of your poem.

continues

'Therefore, to test his patience—
  How much he can endure—
Mention no places, names, or dates,
  And evermore be sure
Throughout the poem to be found
  Consistently obscure.

'First fix upon the limit
  To which it shall extend:
Then fill it up with "Padding"
  (Beg some of any friend):
Your great SENSATION-STANZA
  You place towards the end.'

'And what is a Sensation,
  Grandfather, tell me, pray?
I think I never heard the word
  So used before to-day:
Be kind enough to mention one
  "Exempli gratiâ."'

And the old man, looking sadly
  Across the garden-lawn,
Where here and there a dew-drop
  Yet glittered in the dawn,
Said 'Go to the Adelphi,
  And see the "Colleen Bawn."

'The word is due to Boucicault—
  The theory is his,
Where Life becomes a Spasm,
  And History a Whiz:
If that is not Sensation,
  I don't know what it is.

'Now try your hand, ere Fancy
  Have lost its present glow——'
'And then,' his grandson added,
  'We'll publish it, you know:
Green cloth—gold-lettered at the back—
  In duodecimo!'

Then proudly smiled that old man
  To see the eager lad
Rush madly for his pen and ink
  And for his blotting-pad—
But, when he thought of *publishing,*
  His face grew stern and sad.

Fragment in Imitation of Wordsworth

There is a river clear and fair,
'Tis neither broad nor narrow;
It winds a little here and there—
It winds about like any hare;
And then it takes as straight a course
As on the turnpike road a horse,
  Or through the air an arrow.

The trees that grow upon the shore,
Have grown a hundred years or more;
  So long there is no knowing.
Old Daniel Dobson does not know
When first those trees began to grow;
But still they grew, and grew, and grew,
As if they'd nothing else to do,
  But ever to be growing.

The impulses of air and sky
Have reared their stately stems so high,
  And clothed their boughs with green;
Their leaves the dews of evening quaff,—
  And when the wind blows loud and keen,
I've seen the jolly timbers laugh,

stanza continues

And shake their sides with merry glee—
Wagging their heads in mockery.

Fix'd are their feet in solid earth,
Where winds can never blow;
But visitings of deeper birth
Have reached their roots below.
For they have gained the river's brink,
And of the living waters drink.

There's little Will, a five years' child—
He is my youngest boy;
To look on eyes so fair and wild,
It is a very joy:—
He hath conversed with sun and shower,
And dwelt with every idle flower,
As fresh and gay as them.
He loiters with the briar rose,—
The blue belles are his play-fellows,
That dance upon their slender stem.

And I have said, my little Will,
Why should not he continue still
A thing of Nature's rearing?
A thing beyond the world's control—
A living vegetable soul,—
No human sorrow fearing.

continues

It were a blessed sight to see
That child become a willow tree,
  His brother trees among.
He'd be four times as tall as me,
  And live three times as long.

Miniver Cheevy

Miniver Cheevy, child of scorn,
  Grew lean while he assailed the seasons;
He wept that he was ever born,
  And he had reasons.

Miniver loved the days of old
  When swords were bright and steeds were
    prancing;
The vision of a warrior bold
  Would set him dancing.

Miniver sighed for what was not,
  And dreamed, and rested from his labors;
He dreamed of Thebes and Camelot,
  And Priam's neighbors.

Miniver mourned the ripe renown
  That made so many a name so fragrant;
He mourned Romance, now on the town,
  And Art, a vagrant.

Miniver loved the Medici,
  Albeit he had never seen one;
He would have sinned incessantly
  Could he have been one.

continues

Miniver cursed the commonplace
  And eyed a khaki suit with loathing;
He missed the mediæval grace
  Of iron clothing.

Miniver scorned the gold he sought,
  But sore annoyed was he without it;
Miniver thought, and thought, and thought,
  And thought about it.

Miniver Cheevy, born too late,
  Scratched his head and kept on thinking;
Miniver coughed, and called it fate,
  And kept on drinking.

The Height of the Ridiculous

I wrote some lines once on a time,
In wondrous merry mood,
And thought, as usual, men would say
They were exceeding good.

They were so queer, so very queer,
I laughed as I would die;
Albeit, in the general way,
A sober man am I.

I called my servant, and he came;
How kind it was of him
To mind a slender man like me,
He of the mighty limb.

He took the paper, and I watched,
And saw him peep within;
At the first line he read, his face
Was all upon the grin.

He read the next; the grin grew broad,
And shot from ear to ear;
He read the third; a chuckling noise
I now began to hear.

continues

The fourth, he broke into a roar;
  The fifth, his waistband split;
The sixth, he burst five buttons off,
  And tumbled in a fit.

Ten days and nights, with sleepless eye,
  I watched that wretched man;
And since, I never dare to write
  As funny as I can.

Sonnet Found in a Deserted Mad House

Oh that my soul a marrow-bone might seize!
For the old egg of my desire is broken,
Spilled is the pearly white and spilled the yolk, and
As the mild melancholy contents grease
My path the shorn lamb baas like bumblebees.
Time's trashy purse is as a taken token
Or like a thrilling recitation, spoken
By mournful mouths filled full of mirth and cheese.

And yet, why should I clasp the earthful urn?
Or find the frittered fig that felt the fast?
Or choose to chase the cheese around the churn?
Or swallow any pill from out the past?
Ah, no Love, not while your hot kisses burn
Like a potato riding on the blast.

ANONYMOUS

Hamlet's Soliloquy Imitated

To print, or not to print—that is the question.
Whether 'tis better in a trunk to bury
The quirks and crotchets of outrageous fancy,
Or send a well-wrote copy to the press,
And by disclosing, end them? To print, to doubt
No more; and by one act to say we end
The head-ach, and a thousand natural shocks
Of scribbling frenzy—'tis a consummation
Devoutly to be wish'd. To print—to beam
From the same shelf with Pope, in calf well bound!
To sleep, perchance, with Quarles—Ay there's
the rub—
For to what class a writer may be doom'd,
When he hath shuffled off some paltry stuff,
Must give us pause.—There's the respect that
makes
Th' unwilling poet keep his piece nine years.
For who would bear th' impatient thirst of fame,
The pride of conscious merit, and 'bove all,
The tedious importunity of friends,
When as himself might his quietus make
With a bare inkhorn? Who would fardles bear?
To groan and sweat under a load of wit?
But that the tread of steep Parnassus' hill,
That undiscover'd country, with whose bays
Few travellers return, puzzles the will,

And makes us rather bear to live unknown,
Than run the hazard to be known, and damn'd.
Thus critics do make cowards of us all.
And thus the healthful face of many a poem
Is sickly'd o'er with a pale manuscript;
And enterprisers of great fire, and spirit,
With this regard from Dodsley turn away,
And lose the name of authors.

A Sunnit to the Big Ox

(Composed while standing within two feet of him, and a tuchin' of him now and then.)

All hale! thou mighty annimil—all hale!
You are 4 thousand pounds, and am purty wel
Perporshund, thou tremendjus boveen nuggit!
I wonder how big yu was when yu
Was little, and if yure mother would no yu now
That yu've grone so long, and thick and fat;
Or if yure father would rekognise his ofspring
And his kaff, thou elephanteen quadrupid!
I wonder if it hurts yu much to be so big,
And if yu grode it in a month or so.
I spose wen yu was young tha didn't gin
Yu skim milk but all the creme yu could stuff
Into yore little stummick, jest to see
How big yu'd gro; and afterward tha no doubt
Fed yu on oats and hay and sich like,
With perhaps an occasional punkin or squosh!
In all probability yu don't know yure anny
Bigger than a small kaff; for if yu did
Yude break down fences and switch yure tail,
And rush around and hook and beller,
And run over fowkes, thou orful beast.
O, what a lot of mince pies yude maik,
And sassengers, and your tail,

Whitch can't weigh fur from forty pounds,
Wud maik nigh unto a barrel of ox-tail soup,
And cudn't a heep of staiks be cut off you,
Whitch, with salt and pepper and termater
Ketchup, wouldn't be bad to taik.
Thou grate and glorious inseckt!
But I must close, O most prodijus reptile!
And for mi admiration of yu, when yu di,
I'le rite a node unto yure peddy and remanes,
Pernouncin yu the largest of yure race;
And as I don't expec to have half a dollar
Again to spair for to pay to look at yu, and as
I ain't a dead head, I will sa, farewell.

Lines to a Young Lady

"How pleasant to know Mr. Lear!"
  Who has written such volumes of stuff!
Some think him ill-tempered and queer,
  But a few think him pleasant enough.

His mind is concrete and fastidious,
  His nose is remarkably big;
His visage is more or less hideous,
  His beard it resembles a wig.

He has ears, and two eyes, and ten fingers,
  Leastways if you reckon two thumbs;
Long ago he was one of the singers,
  But now he is one of the dumbs.

He sits in a beautiful parlour,
  With hundreds of books on the wall;
He drinks a great deal of Marsala,
  But never gets tipsy at all.

He has many friends, laymen and clerical,
  Old Foss is the name of his cat;
His body is perfectly spherical,
  He weareth a runcible hat.

When he walks in a waterproof white,
  The children run after him so!
Calling out, "He's come out in his night-
  Gown, that crazy old Englishman, oh!"

He weeps by the side of the ocean,
  He weeps on the top of the hill;
He purchases pancakes and lotion,
  And chocolate shrimps from the mill.

He reads but he cannot speak Spanish,
  He cannot abide ginger-beer:
Ere the days of his pilgrimage vanish,
  How pleasant to know Mr. Lear.

How Pleasant to Ape Mr. Lear

A crusader's wife slipped from the garrison
And had an affair with a Saracen.
  She was not oversexed,
  Or jealous or vexed,
She just wanted to make a comparison.

A novelist of the absurd
Has a voice that will shortly be heard.
  I learn from my spies
  He's about to devise
An unprintable three-letter word.

The Pilgrims ate quahaugs and corn yet,
Which gourmets would scorn through a lorgnette.
  For this kind of living
  They proclaimed a Thanksgiving.
I'm thankful I hadn't been born yet.

An exiled Iraqi went back
To his home with a ewe in his pack.
  He said people all knew
  Every Q needs a U
So he put the ewe back in Iraqu.

A Knight of the Garter long hence
Was expelled from that order of gents.
  He was fairly adroit
  When he cried "Honi Soit,"
But he couldn't pronounce "Mal y Pense."

A chuckling tycoon of Forth Worth,
When asked for the cause of his mirth,
  Replied, Houston and Dallas
  Will shore bust a gallus
When they hear I've just purchased the earth.

A male entomologist author
Waxed wrother and wrother and wrother—
  He socked his own brother
  Who called him a mother
Instead of an eminent mother.

The Spider and the Fly

"Will you walk into my parlor?" said the spider to
the fly;
"'Tis the prettiest little parlor that ever you did spy.
The way into my parlor is up a winding stair,
And I have many pretty things to show when you
are there."
"O no, no," said the little fly, "to ask me is in vain,
For who goes up your winding stair can ne'er come
down again."

"I'm sure you must be weary, dear, with soaring up
so high;
Will you rest upon my little bed?" said the spider to
the fly.
"There are pretty curtains drawn around, the sheets
are fine and thin
And if you like to rest awhile, I'll snugly tuck you in."
"O no, no," said the little fly, "for I've often heard
it said,
They *never, never wake* again, who sleep upon *your* bed."

Said the cunning spider to the fly, "Dear friend,
what shall I do,
To prove the warm affection I've always felt for you?

stanza continues

MARY HOWITT (1799–1888)

I have within my pantry good store of all that's nice;
I'm sure you're very welcome; will you please to take a slice?"
"O no, no," said the little fly, "kind sir, that cannot be;
I've heard what's in your pantry, and I do not wish to see."

"Sweet creature!" said the spider, "You're witty and you're wise,
How handsome are your gauzy wings, how brilliant are your eyes!
I have a little looking-glass upon my parlor shelf,
If you'll step in one moment, dear, you shall behold yourself."
"I thank you, gentle sir," she said, "for what you're pleased to say,
And bidding you good-morning *now,* I'll call *another day.*"

The spider turned him round about, and went into his den,
For well he knew the silly fly would soon be back again:
So he wove a subtle web, in a little corner sly,
And set his table ready to dine upon the fly.

stanza continues

Then he came out to his door again, and merrily
  did sing,
"Come hither, hither, pretty fly, with the pearl and
  silver wing:
Your robes are green and purple; there's a crest
  upon your head;
Your eyes are like the diamond bright, but mine
  are dull as lead."

Alas, alas! how very soon this silly little fly,
Hearing his wily flattering words, came slowly
  flitting by.
With buzzing wings she hung aloft, then near and
  nearer drew,
Thinking only of her brilliant eyes, and green and
  purple hue;
Thinking only of her crested head—*poor foolish
  thing!* At last,
Up jumped the cunning spider, and fiercely held
  her fast.
He dragged her up his winding stair, into his
  dismal den,
Within his little parlor; but she ne'er came out
  again!

And now, dear little children, who may this story read,
To idle, silly, flattering words, I pray you ne'er give heed;
Unto an evil counselor close heart, and ear, and eye,
And take a lesson from this tale of the Spider and the Fly.

MARY HOWITT (1799–1888)

The Duel

The gingham dog and the calico cat
Side by side on the table sat;
'Twas half past twelve, and (what do you think!)
Nor one nor t'other had slept a wink!
  The old Dutch clock and the Chinese plate
  Appeared to know as sure as fate
There was going to be a terrible spat.
  (I wasn't there; I simply state
  What was told to me by the Chinese plate.)

The gingham dog went, "Bow-wow-wow!"
And the calico cat replied, "Mee-ow!"
The air was littered, an hour or so,
With bits of gingham and calico,
  While the old Dutch clock in the chimney place
  Up with its hands before its face,
For it always dreaded a family row.
  (Now mind, I'm only telling you
  What the old Dutch clock declares is true.)

The Chinese plate looked very blue,
And wailed, "Oh, dear! What shall we do?"
But the gingham dog and the calico cat
Wallowed this way and tumbled that,

stanza continues

Employing every tooth and claw
In the awfullest way you ever saw—
And, oh, how the gingham and calico flew!
(Don't fancy I exaggerate;
I got my news from the Chinese plate.)

Next morning, where the two had sat
They found no trace of dog or cat;
And some folks think unto this day
That burglars stole that pair away.
But the truth about the cat and pup
Is this: they ate each other up!
Now what do you really think of that!
(The old Dutch clock, it told me so,
And that is how I came to know.)

EUGENE FIELD (1850–1895)

The Private Dining Room

Miss Rafferty wore taffeta,
Miss Cavendish wore lavender.
We ate pickerel and mackerel
And other lavish provender.
Miss Cavendish was Lalage,
Miss Rafferty was Barbara.
We gobbled pickled mackerel
And broke the candelabara,
Miss Cavendish in lavender,
In taffeta, Miss Rafferty,
The girls in taffeta lavender,
And we, of course, in mufti.

Miss Rafferty wore taffeta,
The taffeta was lavender,
Was lavend, lavender, lavenderest,
As the wine improved the provender.
Miss Cavendish wore lavender,
The lavender was taffeta.
We boggled mackled pickerel,
And bumpers did we quaffeta.
And Lalage wore lavender,
And lavender wore Barbara,
Rafferta taffeta Cavender lavender
Barbara abracadabra.

 OGDEN NASH (1902–1971)

Miss Rafferty in taffeta
Grew definitely raffisher.
Miss Cavendish in lavender
Grew less and less stand-offisher.
With Lalage and Barbara
We grew a little pickereled,
We ordered Mumm and Roederer
Because the bubbles tickereled.
But lavender and taffeta
Were gone when we were soberer.
I haven't thought for thirty years
Of Lalage and Barbara.

Menu

Potage
Potage au Petit Puss.

(Pour Poisson)
Queues de Chat, a l'Anguille.

Ière Entrée
Oreilles de Chat, frites a la
Kilkenny.
Pattes de Chat—aux châtaignes.

zème Entrèe
Cotelettes de petit chat (sauce
doigts de pied de Martyr—
Tomata Sauce).

Roti
Gros Chat Noir.

Pour Légume
De Terre—sans pommes. Petit-
es Pierres cuites à l'eau
chaude.

Gibier

Croquette aux balles.
Canards de Malta.
Sauce au poivre,
Sauce au sel.

Patisserie

Pâté de vers de soie au sucre, breadcrumbs
à l'Oliver Cromwell
(all of a crumble).
Boudin de Mille Mouches.
Compote de Mouches Noires.

The Author Loving these Homely Meats Specially, viz.: Cream, Pancakes, Buttered Pippin-pies (Laugh, Good People) and Tobacco; Writ to that Worthy and Virtuous Gentlewoman, whom He Calleth Mistress, as Followeth

If there were, oh! an Hellespont of cream
Between us, milk-white mistress, I would swim
To you, to show to both my love's extreme,
Leander-like,—yea! dive from brim to brim.
But met I with a buttered pippin-pie
Floating upon 't, that would I make my boat
To waft me to you without jeopardy,
Though sea-sick I might be while it did float.
Yet if a storm should rise, by night or day,
Of sugar-snows and hail of caraways,
Then, if I found a pancake in my way,
It like a plank should bring me to your kays;
  Which having found, if they tobacco kept,
  The smoke should dry me well before I slept.

A Quadrupedremian Song

He dreamt that he saw the Buffalant,
And the spottified Dromedaraffe,
The blue Camelotamus, lean and gaunt,
And the wild Tigeroceros calf.

The maned Liodillo loudly roared,
And the Peccarbok whistled its whine,
The Chinchayak leapt on the dewy sward,
As it hunted the pale Baboopine.

He dreamt that he met the Crocoghau,
As it swam in the Stagnolent Lake;
But everything that in dreams he saw
Came of eating too freely of cake.

Ferdinando and Elvira; Or, the Gentle Pieman

Part I

At a pleasant evening party I had taken down to
supper
One whom I will call ELVIRA, and we talked of love
and TUPPER.

MR. TUPPER and the Poets, very lightly with them
dealing,
For I've always been distinguished for a strong
poetic feeling.

Then we let off paper crackers, each of which
contained a motto,
And she listened while I read them, till her mother
told her not to.

Then she whispered, 'To the ball-room we had
better, dear, be walking;
If we stop down here much longer, really people
will be talking.'

There were noblemen in coronets, and military
cousins,
There were captains by the hundred, there were
baronets by dozens.

Yet she heeded not their offers, but dismissed them
  with a blessing,
Then she let down all her back hair, which had
  taken long in dressing.

Then she had convulsive sobbings in her agitated
  throttle,
Then she wiped her pretty eyes and smelt her
  pretty smelling-bottle.

So I whispered, 'Dear ELVIRA, say,—what can the
  matter be with you?
Does anything you've eaten, darling POPSY, disagree
  with you?'

But spite of all I said, her sobs grew more and more
  distressing,
And she tore her pretty back hair, which had taken
  long in dressing.

Then she gazed upon the carpet, at the ceiling, then
  above me,
And she whispered, 'FERDINANDO, do you really,
  really love me?'

'Love you?' said I, then I sighed, and then I gazed
  upon her sweetly—
For I think I do this sort of thing particularly neatly.

continues

'Send me to the Arctic regions, or illimitable azure,
On a scientific goose-chase, with my COXWELL or
my GLAISHER!

'Tell me whither I may hie me—tell me, dear one,
that I may know—
Is it up the highest Andes? down a horrible volcano?'

But she said, 'It isn't polar bears, or hot volcanic
grottoes:
Only find out who it is that writes those lovely
cracker mottoes!'

Part II

'Tell me, HENRY WADSWORTH, ALFRED, POET CLOSE,
or MISTER TUPPER.
Do you write the bon bon mottoes my ELVIRA pulls
at supper?'

But HENRY WADSWORTH smiled, and said he had
not had that honour;
And ALFRED, too, disclaimed the words that told so
much upon her.

'MISTER MARTIN TUPPER, POET CLOSE, I beg of you
inform us;'
But my question seemed to throw them both into a
rage enormous.

MISTER CLOSE expressed a wish that he could only
get anigh to me;
And MISTER MARTIN TUPPER sent the following
reply to me:

'A fool is bent upon a twig, but wise men dread a
bandit,'—
Which I know was very clever; but I didn't
understand it.

Seven weary years I wandered—Patagonia, China,
Norway,
Till at last I sank exhausted at a pastrycook his
doorway.

There were fuchsias and geraniums, and daffodils
and myrtle,
So I entered, and I ordered half a basin of mock
turtle.

He was plump and he was chubby, he was smooth
and he was rosy,
And his little wife was pretty and particularly cosy.

And he chirped and sang, and skipped about, and
laughed with laughter hearty—
He was wonderfully active for so very stout a party.

continues

And I said, 'O gentle pieman, why so very, very
merry?
Is it purity of conscience, or your one-and-seven
sherry?'

But he answered, 'I'm so happy—no profession
could be dearer—
If I am not humming "Tra! la! la!" I'm singing
"Tirer, lirer!"

'First I go and make the patties, and the puddings,
and the jellies,
Then I make a sugar bird-cage, which upon a table
swell is;

'Then I polish all the silver, which a supper-table
lacquers;
Then I write the pretty mottoes which you find
inside the crackers.'—

'Found at last!' I madly shouted. 'Gentle pieman,
you astound me!'
Then I waved the turtle soup enthusiastically
round me.

And I shouted and I danced until he'd quite a crowd
around him—
And I rushed away exclaiming, 'I have found him!
I have found him!'

And I heard the gentle pieman in the road behind
me trilling,
'"Tira, lira!" stop him, stop him! "Tra! la! la!" the
soup's a shilling!'

But until I reached ELVIRA's home, I never, never
waited,
And ELVIRA to her FERDINAND's irrevocably mated!

An Invitation to Lubberland

There's all sorts of fowl and fish,
  With wine and store of brandy,
Ye have there what your hearts can wish,
  The hills are sugar candy.

There is a ship we understand
  Now riding in the river,
'Tis newly come from Lubberland,
  The like I think was never;
You that a lazy life do love,
  I'd have you now go over,
They say land is not above
  Two thousand leagues from Dover.

The Captain and the Master too
  Do's give us this relation,
And so do's all the whole ship's crew,
  Concerning this strange nation.
The streets are pav'd with pudding-pies,
  Nay powder'd beef and bacon,
They say they scorn to tell you lies,
  Who think it is mistaken.

The king of knaves and queen of sluts
  Reign there in peace and quiet;
You need not fear to starve your guts,
  There is such store of diet;
There you may live free from all care,
  Like hogs set up a fatning,
The garments which the people wear
  Is silver, silk and sattin.

The lofty buildings of this place
  For many years have lasted,
With nutmegs, pepper, cloves and mace
  The walls are roughly casted,
In curious hasty-pudding boil'd,
  And most ingenious carving.
Likewise they are with pancakes ty'd,
  Sure, here's no fear of starving.

The Captain says, in every town
  Hot roasted pigs will meet ye,
They in the streets run up and down,
  Still crying out, come eat me:
Likewise he says, at every feast
  The very fowls and fishes,
Nay, from the biggest to the least,
  Comes tumbling to the dishes.

continues

The rivers run with claret fine,
  The brooks with rich Canary,
The ponds with other sorts of wine,
  To make your hearts full merry:
Nay, more than this, you may behold
  The fountains flow with brandy,
The rocks are like refined gold,
  The hills are sugar candy.

Rosewater is the rain they have
  Which comes in pleasant showers,
All places are adorned brave
  With sweet and fragrant flowers;
Hot custards grow on ev'ry tree,
  Each ditch affords rich jellies.
Now, if you will be rul'd by me,
  Go there, and fill your bellies.

There's nothing there but holy-days,
  With musick out of measure;
Who can forbear to speak the praise
  Of such a land of pleasure?
There you may lead a lazy life,
  Free from all kinds of labour,
And he that is without a wife,
  May borrow of his neighbour.

There is no law, nor lawyers fees,
  All men are free from fury,
For ev'ry one do's what he please,
  Without a judge or jury:
The summer-time is warm they say,
  The winter's ne'er the colder,
They have no landlord's rent to pay,
  Each man is a free-holder.

You that are free to cross the seas,
  Make no more disputation,
At Lubberland you'll live at ease,
  With pleasant recreation:
The captain waits but for a gale,
  Of prosperous wind and weather,
And that they soon will hoist up sail,
  Make haste away together.

"Martin said to his man"

Martin said to his man
  Fie man, fie!
O Martin said to his man
  Who's the fool now?
Martin said to his man
Fill thou the cup and I the can,
Thou hast well drunken, man,
  Who's the fool now?

I see a sheep shearing corn.
  Fie man, fie!
I see a sheep shearing corn.
  Who's the fool now?
I see a sheep shearing corn,
And a cuckold blow his horn.
Thou hast well drunken, man,
  Who's the fool now?

I see a man in the moon.
  Fie man, fie!
I see a man in the moon.
  Who's the fool now?
I see a man in the moon
Clouting of Saint Peter's shoon.
Thou hast well drunken, man,
  Who's the fool now?

I see a hare chase a hound.
  Fie man, fie!
I see a hare chase a hound.
  Who's the fool now?
I see a hare chase a hound
Twenty mile above the ground.
Thou hast well drunken, man,
  Who's the fool now?
I see a goose ring a hog.
  Fie man, fie!

I see a goose ring a hog.
  Who's the fool now?
I see a goose ring a hog.
And a snail that did bite a dog.
Thou hast well drunken, man,
  Who's the fool now?
I see a mouse catch the cat.
  Fie man, fie!

I see a mouse catch the cat.
  Who's the fool now?
I see a mouse catch the cat
And the cheese to eat the rat.
Thou hast well drunken, man,
  Who's the fool now?

"Limericks"

There was an old party of Lyme
Who married three wives at one time.
  When asked: "Why the third?"
  He replied: "One's absurd,
And bigamy, sir, is a crime."

There was a young lady of Niger
Who smiled as she rode on a Tiger;
  They came back from the ride
  With the lady inside,
And the smile on the face of the Tiger.

A wonderful bird is the pelican,
His mouth can hold more than his belican,
  He can take in his beak
  Enough food for a week—
I'm damned if I know how the helican.

There was a young lady named Bright,
Who travelled much faster than light,

stanza continues

She started one day
In the relative way,
And returned on the previous night.

There were two cats of Kilkenny
Each thought there was one too many
So they fought and they fit
And they scratched and they bit
Until there wasn't any.

There was a young fellow of Perth,
Who was born on the day of his birth;
He was married, they say
On his wife's wedding day,
And he died when he quitted the earth.

There was an old fellow of Tring
Who, when somebody asked him to sing,
Replied, "Ain't it odd?
I can never tell *God
Save the Weasel* from *Pop goes the King*."

Pop Goes the Weasel!

Up and down the City Road,
  In and out the Eagle,
That's the way the money goes,
  Pop goes the weasel!

A ha'penny for a cotton ball,
  A farthing for a needle,
That's the way the money goes,
  Pop goes the weasel!

Half a pound of tuppenny rice,
  Half a pound of treacle,
Mix it up and make it nice,
  Pop goes the weasel!

Every time my mother goes out,
  The monkey's on the table,
Cracking nuts and eating spice,
  Pop goes the weasel!

If you want to buy a pig,
  Buy a pig with hairs on,
Every hair a penny a pair,
  Pop goes the weasel!

 W. R. MARDALE (19TH CENTURY)

The little Man that had a little Gun

In stature the Manlet was dwarfish—
 No burly big Blunderbore he:
And he wearily gazed on the crawfish
 His Wifelet had dressed for his tea.
'Now reach me, sweet Atom, my gunlet,
 And hurl the old shoelet for luck:
Let me hie to the bank of the runlet,
  And shoot thee a Duck!'

She has reached him his minikin gunlet:
 She has hurled the old shoelet for luck:
She is busily baking a bunlet,
 To welcome him home with his Duck.
On he speeds, never wasting a wordlet,
 Though thoughtlets cling, closely as wax,
To the spot where the beautiful birdlet
  So quietly quacks.

Where the Lobsterlet lurks, and the Crablet
 So slowly and sleepily crawls:
Where the Dolphin's at home, and the Dablet
 Pays long ceremonious calls:
Where the Grublet is sought by the Froglet:
 Where the Frog is pursued by the Duck:

stanza continues

Where the Ducklet is chased by the Doglet—
So runs the world's luck!

He has loaded with bullet and powder:
His footfall is noiseless as air:
But the Voices grow louder and louder,
And bellow, and bluster, and blare.
They bristle before him and after,
They flutter above and below,
Shrill shriekings of lubberly laughter,
Weird wailings of woe!

They echo without him, within him:
They thrill through his whiskers and beard:
Like a teetotum seeming to spin him,
With sneers never hitherto sneered.
'Avengement,' they cry, 'on our Foelet!
Let the Manikin weep for our wrongs!
Let us drench him, from toplet to toelet,
With Nursery-Songs!

'He shall muse upon "Hey! Diddle! Diddle!"
On the Cow that surmounted the Moon:
He shall rave of the Cat and the Fiddle,
And the Dish that eloped with the Spoon:
And his soul shall be sad for the Spider,
When Miss Muffet was sipping her whey,
That so tenderly sat down beside her,
And scared her away!

'The music of Midsummer-madness
Shall sting him with many a bite,
Till, in rapture of rollicking sadness,
He shall groan with a gloomy delight:
He shall swathe him, like mists of the morning,
In platitudes luscious and limp,
Such as deck, with a deathless adorning,
The Song of the Shrimp!

'When the Ducklet's dark doom is decided,
We will trundle him home in a trice:
And the banquet, so plainly provided,
Shall round into rose-buds and rice:
In a blaze of pragmatic invention
He shall wrestle with Fate, and shall reign:
But he has not a friend fit to mention,
So hit him again!'

He has shot it, the delicate darling!
And the Voices have ceased from their strife:
Not a whisper of sneering or snarling,
As he carries it home to his wife:
Then, cheerily champing the bunlet
His spouse was so skilful to bake,
He hies him once more to the runlet,
To fetch her the Drake!

A Little Man

There was a little man, and he had a little gun,
  And his bullets were made of lead, lead, lead;
He went to the brook, and saw a little duck,
  And shot it right through the head, head, head.

He carried it home to his old wife Joan,
  And bade her a fire to make, make, make.
To roast the little duck he had shot in the brook,
  And he'd go and fetch the drake, drake, drake.

The drake was a-swimming with his curly tail;
  The little man made it his mark, mark, mark.
He let off his gun, but he fired too soon,
  And the drake flew away with a quack,
    quack, quack.

Kindness to Animals

Speak gently to the herring and kindly to the calf,
Be blithesome with the bunny, at barnacles don't
laugh!
Give nuts unto the monkey, and buns unto the bear,
Ne'er hint at currant jelly if you chance to see a
hare!
Oh, little girls, pray hide your combs when
tortoises draw nigh,
And never in the hearing of a pigeon whisper Pie!
But give the stranded jelly-fish a shove into the
sea, —
Be always kind to animals wherever you may be!

Oh, make not game of sparrows, nor faces at
the ram,
And ne'er allude to mint sauce when calling on
a lamb.
Don't beard the thoughtful oyster, don't dare the
cod to crimp,
Don't cheat the pike, or ever try to pot the playful
shrimp.
Tread lightly on the turning worm, don't bruise the
butterfly,
Don't ridicule the wry-neck, nor sneer at salmon-fry;

stanza continues

Oh, ne'er delight to make dogs fight, nor bantams
disagree,—
Be always kind to animals wherever you may be!

Be lenient with lobsters, and ever kind to crabs,
And be not disrespectful to cuttle-fish or dabs;
Chase not the Cochin-China, chaff not the ox obese,
And babble not of feather-beds in company with
geese.
Be tender with the tadpole, and let the limpet
thrive,
Be merciful to mussels, don't skin your eels alive;
When talking to a turtle don't mention calipee—
Be always kind to animals wherever you may be.

Don't Dress Your Cat in an Apron

from *FREE TO BE . . . YOU AND ME*

Don't dress your cat in an apron
Just 'cause he's learning to bake.
Don't put your horse in a nightgown
Just 'cause he can't stay awake.
Don't dress your snake in a muu-muu
Just 'cause he's off on a cruise.
Don't dress your whale in galoshes
If she really prefers overshoes.

A person should wear what he wants to
And not just what other folks say.
A person should do what he likes to—
A person's a person that way.

DAN GREENBURG (B. 1936)

The Pelican Chorus

King and Queen of the Pelicans we;
No other Birds so grand we see!
None but we have feet like fins!
With lovely leathery throats and chins!
  Ploffskin, Pluffskin, Pelican jee!
  We think no Birds so happy as we!
  Plumpskin, Ploshkin, Pelican jill!
  We think so then, and we thought so still!

We live on the Nile. The Nile we love.
By night we sleep on the cliffs above;
By day we fish, and at eve we stand
On long bare islands of yellow sand.
And when the sun sinks slowly down
And the great rock walls grow dark and brown,
Where the purple river rolls fast and dim
And the Ivory Ibis starlike skim,
Wing to wing we dance around,—
Stamping our feet with a flumpy sound,—
Opening our mouths as Pelicans ought,
And this is the song we nightly snort;—
  Ploffskin, Pluffskin, Pelican jee,—
  We think no Birds so happy as we!
  Plumpskin, Ploshkin, Pelican jill,—
  We think so then, and we thought so still.

Last year came out our Daughter, Dell;
And all the Birds received her well.
To do her honour, a feast we made
For every bird that can swim or wade.
Herons and Gulls, and Cormorants black,
Cranes, and Flamingoes with scarlet back,
Plovers and Storks, and Geese in clouds,
Swans and Dilberry Ducks in crowds.
Thousands of Birds in wondrous flight!
They ate and drank and danced all night,
And echoing back from the rocks you heard
Multitude-echoes from Bird and Bird,—
  Ploffskin, Pluffskin, Pelican jee,
  We think no Birds so happy as we!
  Plumpskin, Ploshkin, Pelican jill,
  We think so then, and we thought so still!

Yes, they came; and among the rest,
The King of the Cranes all grandly dressed.
Such a lovely tail! Its feathers float
Between the ends of his blue dress-coat;
With pea-green trowsers all so neat,
And a delicate frill to hide his feet,—
(For though no one speaks of it, every one knows,
He has got no webs between his toes!)
As soon as he saw our Daughter Dell,
In violent love that Crane King fell,—

stanza continues

On seeing her waddling form so fair,
With a wreath of shrimps in her short white hair.
And before the end of the next long day,
Our Dell had given her heart away;
For the King of the Cranes had won that heart,
With a Crocodile's egg and a large fish-tart.
She vowed to marry the King of the Cranes,
Leaving the Nile for stranger plains;
And away they flew in a gathering crowd
Of endless birds in a lengthening cloud.
  Ploffskin, Pluffskin, Pelican jee,
  We think no Birds so happy as we!
  Plumpskin, Ploshkin, Pelican jill,
  We think so then, and we thought so still!

And far away in the twilight sky,
We heard them singing a lessening cry,—
Farther and farther till out of sight,
And we stood alone in the silent night!
Often since, in the nights of June,
We sit on the sand and watch the moon;—
She has gone to the great Gromboolian plain,
And we probably never shall meet again!
Oft, in the long still nights of June,
We sit on the rocks and watch the moon;—
——She dwells by the streams of the Chankly Bore,
And we probably never shall see her more.

stanza continues

Ploffskin, Pluffskin, Pelican jee,
We think no Birds so happy as we!
Plumpskin, Ploshkin, Pelican jill,
We think so then, and we thought so still!

"Lawn as white as driven snow;"

from *THE WINTER'S TALE*

Lawn as white as driven snow;
Cyprus black as e'er was crow;
Gloves as sweet as damask roses;
Masks for faces and for noses;
Bugle-bracelet, necklace-amber,
Perfume for a lady's chamber;
Golden quoifs and stomachers,
For my lads to give their dears;
Pins and poking-sticks of steel,
What maids lack from head to heel:
Come buy of me, come; come buy, come buy;
Buy, lads, or else your lasses cry:
Come buy.

The Derby Ram

As I was going to Derby,
'Twas on a market day,
I saw the finest ram, sir,
That ever was fed on hay.
This ram was fat behind, sir,
This ram was fat before,
This ram was ten yards high, sir,
If he wasn't a little more.
That's a lie, that's a lie,
That's a tid i fa la lie.

Now the inside of this ram, sir,
Would hold ten sacks of corn,
And you could turn a coach and six
On the inside of his horn.
Now the wool upon his back, sir,
It reached up to the sky,
And in it was a crow's nest,
For I heard the young ones cry.
That's a lie, that's a lie,
That's a tid i fa la lie.

Now the wool upon his belly, sir,
Went draggling on the ground,

stanza continues

And that was took to Derby, sir,
  And sold for ten thousand pound.
Now the wool upon his tail, sir,
  Was ten inches and an ell,
And that was took to Derby, sir,
  To toll the old market-bell.
      That's a lie, that's a lie,
      That's a tid i fa la lie.

Now the man that fed this ram, sir,
  He fed him twice a day,
And each time he fed him, sir,
  He ate a rick of hay.
Now the man that watered this ram, sir,
  He watered him twice a day,
And each time that he watered him
  He drank the river dry.
      That's a lie, that's a lie,
      That's a tid i fa la lie.

Now the butcher that killed the ram, sir,
  Was up to his knees in blood,
And the boy that held the bowl, sir,
  Got washed away in the flood.
Now all the boys in Derby, sir,
  Went begging for his eyes,

stanza continues

They kicked them up and down the street,
  For they were a good football size.
    That's a lie, that's a lie,
    That's a tid i fa la lie.

Now all the women of Derby, sir,
  Went begging for his ears,
To make their leather aprons of
  That lasted them forty years.
And the man that fatted the ram, sir,
  He must be very rich,
And the man that sung this song, sir,
  Is a lying son of a bitch.
    That's the truth, that's the truth,
    That's the tid i fa la truth.

The Parrot

Palma Kunkel's parrot proves
showing off is for the birds.
No known situation moves
him to utter any words.

Words he hoards, so their extent
can't be measured fruitfully.
Smartest bird for sale or rent:
breeding's very apogee.

Casting a cold eye upon you,
tongue retracted in his beak—
whatever topic you get on to,
not a single word he'll speak.

Translated from the German by
Stuart Miller (b. 1949)

Dame Wiggins of Lee and her Seven Wonderful Cats

Dame Wiggins of Lee
Was a worthy old soul,
As e'er threaded a nee-
dle, or wash'd in a bowl:
She held mice and rats
In such antipa-thy
That seven fine cats
Kept Dame Wiggins of Lee.

The rats and mice scared
By this fierce whisker'd crew,
The seven poor cats
Soon had nothing to do;
So, as any one idle
She ne'er loved to see,
She sent them to school,
Did Dame Wiggins of Lee.

But soon she grew tired
Of living alone;
So she sent for her cats
From school to come home.

stanza continues

Each rowing a wherry,
Returning you see:
The frolic made merry
Dame Wiggins of Lee.

The Dame was quite pleas'd,
And ran out to market;
When she came back
They were mending the carpet.
The needle each handled
As brisk as a bee;
'Well done, my good cats,'
Said Dame Wiggins of Lee.

To give them a treat,
She ran out for some rice;
When she came back,
They were skating on ice.
'I shall soon see one drown,
Aye, perhaps, two or three,
I'll bet half-a-crown,'
Said Dame Wiggins of Lee.

They called the next day
On the tomtit and sparrow,
And wheeled a poor sick lamb
Home in a barrow.

stanza continues

'You shall all have some sprats
For your human-ity,
My seven good cats,'
Said Dame Wiggins of Lee.

While she ran to the fields,
To look for its dam,
They were warming the bed
For the poor sick lamb:
They'd turned up the clothes
All as neat as could be;
'I shall ne'er want a nurse,'
Said Dame Wiggins of Lee.

She wished them good night,
And went up to bed;
When, lo! in the morning,
The cats were all fled.
But soon—what a fuss!
'Where can they all be?
Here, pussy, puss, puss!'
Cried Dame Wiggins of Lee.

The Dame's heart was nigh broke,
So she sat down to weep,
When she saw them come back
Each riding a sheep;

stanza continues

She fondled and patted
Each purring Tom-my:
'Ah! welcome, my dears,'
Said Dame Wiggins of Lee.

The Dame was unable
Her pleasure to smother;
To see the sick Lamb
Jump up to its mother
In spite of the gout,
And a pain in her knee,
She went dancing about:
Did Dame Wiggins of Lee.

The Farmer soon heard
Where his sheep went astray,
And arrived at Dame's door
With his faithful dog Tray.
He knocked with his crook,
And the stranger to see,
Out of window did look
Dame Wiggins of Lee.

For their kindness he had them
All drawn by his team;
And gave them some field-mice,
And raspberry-cream.

stanza continues

Said he, 'All my stock
You shall presently see;
For I honour the cats
Of Dame Wiggins of Lee.'

He set his maid out
For some muffins and crumpets;
And when he turn'd round
They were playing of trumpets.
Said he, 'I suppose,
She's as deaf as can be,
Or this ne'er could be born
By Dame Wiggins of Lee.'

To show them his poultry,
He turn'd them all loose,
When each nimbly leap'd
On the back of a Goose,
Which frighten'd them so
That they ran to the sea,
And half-drown'd the poor cats
Of Dame Wiggins of Lee.

For their care of his lamb,
And their comical pranks,
He gave them a ham
And abundance of thanks.

stanza continues

'I wish you good-day,
My fine fellows,' said he:
'My compliments, pray,
To Dame Wiggins of Lee.'

You see them arrived
At their Dame's welcome door;
They show her their presents,
And all their good store.
'Now come in to supper,
And sit down with me;
All welcome once more,'
Cried Dame Wiggins of Lee.

The Owl and the Pussy-Cat

The Owl and the Pussy-Cat went to sea
 In a beautiful pea-green boat:
They took some honey, and plenty of money
 Wrapped up in a five-pound note.
The Owl looked up to the stars above,
 And sang to a small guitar,
"Oh, lovely Pussy, oh, Pussy, my love,
 What a beautiful Pussy you are,
  You are,
  You are!
 What a beautiful Pussy you are!"

Pussy said to the Owl, "You elegant fowl,
 How charmingly sweet you sing!
Oh, let us be married; too long we have tarried:
 But what shall we do for a ring?"
They sailed away for a year and a day,
 To the land where the bong-tree grows;
And there in the wood a Piggy-wig stood,
 With a ring at the end of his nose,
  His nose,
  His nose,
 With a ring at the end of his nose.

continues

"Dear Pig, are you willing to sell for one shilling
  Your ring?" Said the Piggy, "I will."
So they took it away and were married next day
  By the Turkey who lives on the hill.
They dined on mince and slices of quince,
  Which they ate with a runcible spoon;
And hand in hand, on the edge of the sand,
  They danced by the light of the moon,
        The moon,
        The moon,
  They danced by the light of the moon.

EDWARD LEAR (1812–1888)

I Saw a Peacock

I saw a peacock with a fiery tail
I saw a blazing comet pour down hail
I saw a cloud all wrapt with ivy round
I saw a lofty oak creep on the ground
I saw a beetle swallow up a whale
I saw a foaming sea brimful of ale
I saw a pewter cup sixteen feet deep
I saw a well full of men's tears that weep
I saw wet eyes in flames of living fire
I saw a house as high as the moon and higher
I saw the glorious sun at deep midnight
I saw the man who saw this wondrous sight.

ANONYMOUS

The Purple Cow

I never saw a Purple cow,
I never hope to see one;
But I can tell you, anyhow,
I'd rather see than be one.

Confession

Ah, yes! I wrote the "Purple Cow"—
I'm Sorry, now, I Wrote it.
But I can Tell you Anyhow,
I'll Kill you if you Quote it.

The Monkey's Glue

When the monkey in his madness
  Took the glue to mend his voice,
'Twas the crawfish showed his sadness
  That the bluebird could rejoice.

Then the perspicacious parrot
  Sought to save the suicide
By administering carrot,
  But the monkey merely died.

So the crawfish and the parrot
  Sauntered slowly toward the sea,
While the bluebird stole the carrot
  And returned the glue to me.

GOLDWIN GOLDSMITH (1728–1774)

"Queen Mab"

from *ROMEO AND JULIET*

MERCUTIO O, then, I see Queen Mab hath been with you.
She is the fairies' midwife, and she comes
In shape no bigger than an agate-stone
On the fore-finger of an alderman,
Drawn with a team of little atomies
Athwart men's noses as they lie asleep;
Her waggon-spokes made of long spinners' legs,
The cover of the wings of grasshoppers,
The traces of the smallest spider's web,
The collars of the moonshine's watery beams,
Her whip of cricket's bone, the lash of film,
Her waggoner a small grey-coated gnat,
Not half so big as a round little worm
Prick'd from the lazy finger of a maid;
Her chariot is an empty hazel-nut
Made by the joiner squirrel or old grub,
Time out o' mind the fairies' coachmakers.
And in this state she gallops night by night
Through lovers' brains, and then they dream of love;
O'er courtiers' knees, that dream on court'sies straight,
O'er lawyers' fingers, who straight dream on fees,
O'er ladies' lips, who straight on kisses dream,

Which oft the angry Mab with blisters plagues,
Because their breaths with sweetmeats tainted are:
Sometime she gallops o'er a courtier's nose,
And then dreams he of smelling out a suit;
And sometime comes she with a tithe-pig's tail
Tickling a parson's nose as a' lies asleep,
Then dreams he of another benefice:
Sometime she driveth o'er a soldier's neck,
And then dreams he of cutting foreign throats,
Of breaches, ambuscadoes, Spanish blades,
Of healths five-fathom deep; and then anon
Drums in his ear, at which he starts and wakes,
And being thus frighted, swears a prayer or two
And sleeps again. This is that very Mab
That plats the manes of horses in the night,
And bakes the elf-locks in foul sluttish hairs,
Which once untangled much misfortune bodes:
This is the hag, when maids lie on their backs,
That presses them and learns them first to bear,
Making them women of good carriage:
This is she—
ROMEO Peace, peace, Mercutio, peace!
Thou talk'st of nothing.
MERCUTIO True, I talk of dreams,
Which are the children of an idle brain,
Begot of nothing but vain fantasy,
Which is as thin of substance as the air

continues

And more inconstant than the wind, who wooes
Even now the frozen bosom of the north,
And, being anger'd, puffs away from thence,
Turning his face to the dew-dropping south.

The Mad Gardener's Song

He thought he saw an Elephant,
  That practised on a fife:
He looked again, and found it was
  A letter from his wife.
'At length I realise,' he said,
  'The bitterness of Life!'

He thought he saw a Buffalo
  Upon the chimney-piece:
He looked again, and found it was
  His Sister's Husband's Niece,
'Unless you leave this house,' he said,
  'I'll send for the Police!'

He thought he saw a Rattlesnake
  That questioned him in Greek:
He looked again, and found it was
  The Middle of Next Week.
'The one thing I regret,' he said,
  'Is that it cannot speak!'

He thought he saw a Banker's Clerk
  Descending from the bus:
He looked again, and found it was

stanza continues

A Hippopotamus:
'If this should stay to dine,' he said,
'There won't be much for us!'

He thought he saw a Kangaroo
That worked a coffee-mill:
He looked again, and found it was
A Vegetable-Pill.
'Were I to swallow this,' he said,
'I should be very ill!'

He thought he saw a Coach-and-Four
That stood beside his bed:
He looked again, and found it was
A Bear without a Head.
'Poor thing,' he said, 'poor silly thing!
It's waiting to be fed!'

He thought he saw an Albatross
That fluttered round the lamp:
He looked again, and found it was
A Penny-Postage-Stamp.
'You'd best be getting home,' he said:
'The nights are very damp!'

He thought he saw a Garden-Door
  That opened with a key:
He looked again, and found it was
  A Double Rule of Three:
'And all its mystery,' he said,
  'Is clear as day to me!'

He thought he saw an Argument
  That proved he was the Pope:
He looked again, and found it was
  A Bar of Mottled Soap.
'A fact so dread,' he faintly said,
  'Extinguishes all hope!'

The Picket Fence

There was a picket fence with blank
space to peer between each plank.

A passing architect who spied it
stopped short one evening right beside it,

extracted all the space and built
a mansion with it—to the hilt.

The pickets languished there, dumbfounded.
Not one had spaces to surround it:

a sight so sickening, the town
condemned the mess and tore it down.

The architect left in a hurry
for Londondu, or Katmanderry.

Translated from the German by
Stuart Miller (b. 1949)

Impromptu

If I were a cassowary
  On the plains of Timbuctoo,
I would eat a missionary,
  Cassock, bands and hymn-book too.

SAMUEL WILBERFORCE (1805–1873)

Scientific Proof

If we square a lump of pemmican
  And cube a pot of tea,
Divide a musk ox by the span
  From noon to half-past three;
If we calculate the Eskimo
  By solar parallax,
Divide the sextant by a floe
  And multiply the cracks
By *n*th-powered igloos, we may prove
  All correlated facts.

If we prolongate the parallel
  Indefinitely forth,
And cube a sledge till we can tell
  The real square root of North;
Bisect a seal and bifurcate
  The tangent with a pack
Of Polar ice, we get the rate
  Along the Polar track,
And proof of corollary things
  Which otherwise we lack.

If we multiply the Arctic night
  By X times ox times moose,

stanza continues

And build an igloo on the site
Of its hypotenuse;
If we circumscribe an arc about
An Arctic dog and weigh
A segment of it, every doubt
Is made as clear as day,
We also get the price of ice
F.O.B. Baffin's Bay.

If we amplify the Arctic breeze
By logarithmic signs,
And run through the isosceles
Imaginary lines,
We find that twice the half of one
Is equal to the whole.
Which, when the calculus is done,
Quite demonstrates the Pole.
It also gives its length and breadth
And what's the price of coal.

J. W. FOLEY (1874–1939)

Song of the Screw

A moving form or rigid mass,
  Under whate'er conditions
Along successive screws must pass
  Between each two positions.
It turns around and slides along—
This is the burden of my song.

The pitch of screw, if multiplied
  By angle of rotation,
Will give the distance it must glide
  In motion of translation.
Infinite pitch means pure translation,
And zero pitch means pure rotation.

Two motions on two given screws,
  With amplitudes at pleasure,
Into a third screw-motion fuse;
  Whose amplitude we measure
By parallelogram construction
(A very obvious deduction.)

Its axis cuts the nodal line
  Which to both screws is normal,
And generates a form divine,
  Whose name, in language formal,

stanza continues

Is "surface-ruled of third degree."
Cylindroid is the name for me.

Rotation round a given line
  Is like a force along.
If to say couple you incline,
  You're clearly in the wrong; —
'Tis obvious, upon reflection,
A line is not a mere direction.

So couples with translations too
  In all respects agree;
And thus there centres in the screw
  A wondrous harmony
Of Kinematics and of Statics, —
The sweetest thing in mathematics.

The forces on one given screw,
  With motion on a second,
In general some work will do,
  Whose magnitude is reckoned
By angle, force, and what we call
The coefficient virtual.

Rotation now to force convert,
  And force into rotation;
Unchanged the work, we can assert,

stanza continues

In spite of transformation.
And if two screws no work can claim,
Reciprocal will be their name.

Five numbers will a screw define,
A screwing motion, six;
For four will give the axial line,
One more the pitch will fix;
And hence we always can contrive
One screw reciprocal to five.

Screws—two, three, four or five, combined
(No question here of six),
Yield other screws which are confined
Within one screw complex.
Thus we obtain the clearest notion
Of freedom and constraint of motion.

In complex III., three several screws
At every point you find,
Or if you one direction choose,
One screw is to your mind;
And complexes of order III.
Their own reciprocals may be.

In IV., wherever you arrive,
You find of screws a cone,

stanza continues

On every line in complex V.
  There is precisely one;
At each point of this complex rich,
A plane of screws have given pitch.

But time would fail me to discourse
  Of Order and Degree;
Of Impulse, Energy and Force,
  And Reciprocity.
All these and more, for motions small,
Have been discussed by Dr. Ball.

"Clerihews"

It was rather disconcerting for Hannibal
To be introduced to a cannibal
Who expressed the very highest opinion
Of cold pickled Carthaginian.

"I quite realized," said Columbus,
"That the Earth was not a rhombus,
"But I *am* a little annoyed
"To find it an oblate spheroid."

Edgar Allan Poe
Was passionately fond of roe.
He always liked to chew some
When writing anything gruesome.

The Art of Biography
Is different from Geography.
Geography is about Maps,
But Biography is about Chaps.

A Love-Song by a Lunatic

There's not a spider in the sky,
  There's not a glowworm in the sea,
There's not a crab that soars on high,
  But bids me dream, dear maid, of thee!

When watery Phœbus ploughs the main,
  When fiery Luna gilds the lea,
As flies run up the window-pane,
  So fly my thoughts, dear love, to thee!

ANONYMOUS

To Marie

When the breeze from the bluebottle's blustering
blim
Twirls the toads in a tooroomaloo,
And the whiskery whine of the wheedlesome whim
Drowns the roll of the rattatattoo,
Then I dream in the shade of the shally-go-shee,
And the voice of the bally-molay
Brings the smell of the pale poppy-cod's blummered
blee
From the willy-wad over the way.

Ah, the shuddering shoe and the blinketty-blanks
When the punglung falls from the bough
In the blast of a hurricane's hicketty-hanks
O'er the hills of the hocketty-how!
Give the rigamarole to the clangery-whang,
If they care for such fiddlededee;
But the thingumbob kiss of the whangery-bang
Keeps the higgledly-piggle for me.

L'ENVOI

It is pilly-po-doddle and aligobung
When the lollypup covers the ground,

stanza continues

Yet the poldiddle perishes plunkety-pung
  When the heart jimny-coggles around.
If the soul cannot snoop at the gigglesome cart
  Seeking surcease in gluggety-glug,
It is useless to say to the pulsating heart,
  "Yankee-doodle ker-chuggety-chug!"

Lydia, The Tattooed Lady

Lydia, oh! Lydia, say have you met Lydia,
Oh! Lydia, The Tattooed Lady,
She has eyes that folks adore so.
And a torso even more so.
Lydia, oh! Lydia, that 'Encyclopedia,'
Oh! Lydia, the Queen of tattoo.
On her back is the Battle of Waterloo,
Beside it the Wreck of the Hesperus too,
And proudly above waves the Red, White, and Blue,
You can learn a lot from Lydia.
La-la-la…la-la-la
La-la-la…la-la-la.
She can give you a view of the world in tattoo if
you step up and tell her where.
For a dime you can see Kankakee or Paree, or
Washington crossing the Delaware.
Oh! Lydia, oh! Lydia, say, have you met Lydia,
Oh! Lydia, The Tattooed Lady.
When her muscles start relaxin'
Up the hill comes Andrew Jackson.
Lydia, oh! Lydia, that 'Encyclopedia'
Oh! Lydia, the champ of them all.
For two bits she will do a Mazurka in Jazz,
With a view of Niag'ra that no artist has,
And on a clear day you can see Alcatraz,
You can learn a lot from Lydia.

La-la-la...la-la-la.
La-la-la...la-la-la.
Come along and see Buff'lo Bill with his lasso,
Just a little classic by Mendel Picasso;
Here is Captain Spaulding exploring the Amazon,
And Godiva, but with her pajamas on.
La-la-la...la-la-la.
La-la-la...la-la-la.
Here is Grover Whalen unveilin' the Trylon,
Over on the west coast we have Treasure Islan',
Here's Nijinsky a doin' the Rhumba,
Here's her Social Security numba.
La-la-la...la-la-la.
La-la-la...la-la-la.
Lydia, oh! Lydia, have you met Lydia,
Oh! Lydia, the champ of them all.
She once swept an Admiral clear off his feet,
The ships on her hips made his heart skip a beat,
And now the old boy's in command of the fleet,
For he went and married Lydia.

from Ralph Roister Doister

I mun be married a Sunday,
I mun be married a Sunday,
Whosoever shall come that way,
I mun be married a Sunday.

Roister Doister is my name,
Roister Doister is my name,
A lusty brute I am the same,
I mun be married a Sunday.

Christian Custance have I found,
Christian Custance have I found,
A widow worth a thousand pound,
I mun be married a Sunday.

Custance is as sweet as honey,
Custance is as sweet as honey,
I her lamb and she my coney,
I mun be married a Sunday.

When we shall make our wedding feast,
When we shall make our wedding feast,
There shall be cheer for man and beast,
I mun be married a Sunday.
I mun be married a Sunday,
Whoever shall come that way,
I mun be married a Sunday.

NICHOLAS UDALL (1505–1556)

A Letter to Evelyn Baring

Thrippsy pillivinx,

Inky tinky pobbleboskle abblesquabs? — Flosky! beebul trimble flosky! — Okul scratchabibblebongibo, viddle squibble tog-a-tog, ferrymoyassity amsky flamsky ramsky damsky crocklefether squiggs.

Flinkywisty pomm,
Slushypipp

"flotsam and jetsam"

flotsam and jetsam
are gentlemen poeds
urseappeal netsam
our spinsters and coeds)

thoroughly bretish
they scout the inhuman
itarian fetish
that man isn't wuman

vive the millenni
um three cheers for labor
give all things to enni
one bugger thy nabor

(neck and senecktie
are gentlemen ppoyds
even whose recktie
are covered by lloyd's

Oh, Hollow! Hollow! Hollow!

What time the poet hath hymned
The writhing maid, lithe-limbed,
  Quivering on amaranthine asphodel,
How can he paint her woes,
Knowing, as well he knows,
  That all can be set right with calomel?

When from the poet's plinth
The amorous colocynth
  Yearns for the aloe, faint with rapturous thrills,
How can he hymn their throes,
Knowing, as well he knows,
  That they are only uncompounded pills?

Is it, and can it be,
Nature hath this decree,
  Nothing poetic in the world shall dwell?
Or that in all her works
Something poetic lurks,
  Even in colocynth and calomel?
    I cannot tell.

W. S. GILBERT (1836–1911)

"Puck's Song"

from *A MIDSUMMER NIGHT'S DREAM*

On the ground
Sleep sound:
I'll apply
To your eye,
Gentle lover, remedy.
When thou wakest,
Thou takest
True delight
In the sight
Of thy former lady's eye:
And the country proverb known,
That every man should take his own,
In your waking shall be shown:
Jack shall have Jill;
Naught shall go ill;
The man shall have his mare again, and all
shall be well.

Jack and Jill

Jack and Jill
Went up the hill
To fetch a pail of water.

Jack fell down
And broke his crown
And Jill came tumbling after.

Ipecacuanha

Coughing in a shady grove
  Sat my Juliana,
Lozenges I gave my love,
  Ipecacuanha—
Full twenty from the lozenge box
  The greedy nymph did pick;
Then, sighing sadly, said to me—
  My Damon, I am sick.

Bantams in Pine-Woods

Chieftain Iffucan of Azcan in caftan
Of tan with henna hackles, halt!

Damned universal cock, as if the sun
Was blackamoor to bear your blazing tail.

Fat! Fat! Fat! Fat! I am the personal.
Your world is you. I am my world.

You ten-foot poet among inchlings. Fat!
Begone! An inchling bristles in these pines,

Bristles, and points their Appalachian tangs,
And fears not portly Azcan nor his hoos.

Sally Simpkin's Lament or, John Jones's Kit-cat-astrophe

'Oh! what is that comes gliding in,
  And quite in middling haste?
It is the picture of my Jones,
  And painted to the waist.

'It is not painted to the life,
  For where's the trowsers blue?
Oh Jones, my dear! — Oh dear! my Jones,
  What is become of you?'

'Oh! Sally dear, it is too true, —
  The half that you remark
Is come to say my other half
  Is bit off by a shark!

'Oh! Sally, sharks do things by halves,
  Yet most completely do!
A bite in one place seems enough,
  But I've been bit in two.

'You know I once was all your own,
  But now a shark must share!
But let that pass — for now to you
  I'm neither here nor there.

'Alas! death has a strange divorce
  Effected in the sea,
It has divided me from you,
  And even me from me!

'Don't fear my ghost will walk o' nights
  To haunt as people say;
My ghost *can't* walk, for, oh! my legs
  Are many leagues away!

'Lord! think when I am swimming round,
  And looking where the boat is,
A shark just snaps away a *half*,
  Without "a *quarter*'s notice".

'One half is here, the other half
  Is near Columbia placed;
Oh! Sally, I have got the whole
  Atlantic for my waist.

'But now, adieu—a long adieu!
  I've solved death's awful riddle,
And would say more, but I am doomed
  To break off in the middle.'

The Chancellor's Nightmare

Love, unrequited, robs me of my rest:
Love, hopeless love, my ardent soul encumbers:
Love, nightmare-like, lies heavy on my chest:
And weaves itself into my midnight slumbers!

When you're lying awake with a dismal headache,
and repose is taboo'd by anxiety,
I conceive you may use any language you choose to
indulge in, without impropriety;
For your brain is on fire—the bedclothes conspire
of usual slumber to plunder you:
First your counterpane goes, and uncovers your toes,
and your sheet slips demurely from under you;
Then the blanketing tickles—you feel like mixed
pickles—so terribly sharp is the pricking.
And you're hot, and you're cross, and you tumble
and toss till there's nothing 'twixt you and the
ticking.
Then the bedclothes all creep to the ground in a
heap, and you pick 'em all up in a tangle;
Next your pillow resigns and politely declines to
remain at its usual angle!
Well, you get some repose in the form of a doze,
with hot eyeballs and head ever aching,

But your slumbering teems with such horrible
  dreams that you'd very much better be waking;
For you dream you are crossing the Channel, and
  tossing about in a steamer from Harwich—
Which is something between a large bathing
  machine and a very small second-class carriage—
And you're giving a treat (penny ice and cold meat)
  to a party of friends and relations—
They're a ravenous horde—and they all came on
  board at Sloane Square and South Kensington
  Stations.
And bound on that journey you find your attorney
  (who started that morning from Devon);
He's a bit undersized, and you don't feel surprised
  when he tells you he's only eleven.
Well, you're driving like mad with this singular lad
  (by the by, the ship's now a four-wheeler),
And you're playing round games, and he calls you
  bad names when you tell him that 'ties pay the
  dealer';
But this you can't stand, so you throw up your
  hand, and you find you're as cold as an icicle,
In your shirt and your socks (the black silk with
  gold clocks), crossing Salisbury Plain on a
  bicycle:

continues

And he and the crew are on bicycles too—which
they've somehow or other invested in—
And he's telling the tars all the particu*lars* of a
company he's interested in—
It's a scheme of devices, to get at low prices all
goods from cough mixtures to cables
(Which tickled the sailors,) by treating retailers as
though they were all vege*ta*bles—
You get a good spadesman to plant a small tradesman
(first take off his boots with a boot-tree),
And his legs will take root, and his fingers will shoot,
and they'll blossom and bud like a fruit-tree—
From the greengrocer tree you get grapes and
green pea, cauliflower, pineapple, and
cranberries,
While the pastrycook plant cherry brandy will grant,
apple puffs, and three-corners, and Banburys—
The shares are a penny, and ever so many are taken
by Rothschild and Baring,
And just as a few are allotted to you, you awake
with a shudder despairing—
You're a regular wreck, with a crick in your neck,
and no wonder you snore, for your head's on the
floor, and you've needles and pins from your
soles to your shins, and your flesh is a-creep, for
your left leg's asleep, and you've cramp in your

toes, and a fly on your nose, and a thirst that's intense, and a general sense that you haven't been sleeping in clover;
But the darkness has passed, and it's daylight at last, and the night has been long—ditto ditto my song—and thank goodness they're both of them over!

Brian O'Linn

Brian O'Linn was a gentleman born,
His hair it was long and his beard unshorn,
His teeth were out and his eyes far in—
'I'm a wonderful beauty,' says Brian O'Linn!

Brian O'Linn was hard up for a coat,
He borrowed the skin of a neighbouring goat,
He buckled the horns right under his chin—
'They'll answer for pistols,' says Brian O'Linn!

Brian O'Linn had no breeches to wear,
He got him a sheepskin to make him a pair,
With the fleshy side out and the woolly side in—
'They are pleasant and cool,' says Brian O'Linn!

Brian O'Linn had no hat to his head,
He stuck on a pot that was under the shed,
He murdered a cod for the sake of his fin—
' 'Twill pass for a feather,' says Brian O'Linn!

Brian O'Linn had no shirt to his back,
He went to a neighbour and borrowed a sack.
He puckered a meal-bag under his chin—
'They'll take it for ruffles,' says Brian O'Linn!

Brian O'Linn had no shoes at all,
He bought an old pair at a cobbler's stall,
The uppers were broke and the soles were thin—
'They'll do me for dancing,' says Brian O'Linn!

Brian O'Linn had no watch for to wear,
He bought a fine turnip and scooped it out fair,
He slipped a live cricket right under the skin—
'They'll think it is ticking,' says Brian O'Linn!

Brian O'Linn was in want of a brooch,
He stuck a brass pin in a big cockroach,
The breast of his shirt he fixed it straight in—
'They'll think it's a diamond,' says Brian O'Linn!

Brian O'Linn went a-courting one night,
He set both the mother and daughter to fight—
'Stop, stop,' he exclaimed, 'if you have but the tin,
I'll marry you both,' says Brian O'Linn!

Brian O'Linn went to bring his wife home,
He had but one horse, that was all skin and bone—
'I'll put her behind me, as nate as a pin,
And her mother before me,' says Brian O'Linn!

Brian O'Linn and his wife and wife's mother,
They all crossed over the bridge together,
The bridge broke down and they all tumbled in—
'We'll go home by water,' says Brian O'Linn!

ANONYMOUS

Epigram

As Thomas was cudgell'd one day by his wife,
He took to the street, and fled for his life:
Tom's three dearest friends came by in the squabble,
And saved him at once from the shrew and the
  rabble;
Then ventured to give him some sober advice—
But Tom is a person of honour so nice,
Too wise to take counsel, too proud to take warning,
That he sent to all three a challenge next morning.
Three duels he fought, thrice ventur'd his life;
Went home, and was cudgell'd again by his wife.

Gae out and bar the door

It fell about the Martinmas time,
  And a gay time it was then,
When our goodwife got puddings to make,
  She's boil'd them in the pan.

The wind sae cauld blew south and north,
  And blew into the floor;
Quoth our goodman to our goodwife,
  "Gae out and bar the door."

"My hand is in the hussyfskap,
  Goodman, as ye may see;
An it shoud nae be barr'd this hundred year,
  It's no be barr'd for me."

They made a paction 'tween them twa,
  They made it firm and sure,
That the first word whae'er shou'd speak,
  Shoud rise and bar the door.

Then by there came two gentlemen,
  At twelve o'clock at night,
And they could neither see house nor hall,
  Nor coal nor candle-light.

continues

"Now whether is this a rich man's house,
Or whether it is a poor?"
But ne'er a word wad ane o' them speak,
For barring of the door.

And first they ate the white puddings,
And then they ate the black;
Tho' muckle thought the goodwife to hersel',
Yet ne'er a word she spake.

Then said the one unto the other,
"Here, man, tak ye my knife;
Do ye tak aff the auld man's beard,
And I'll kiss the goodwife."

"But there's nae water in the house,
And what shall we do than?"
"What ails ye at the pudding broo,
That boils into the pan?"

O up then started our goodman,
An angry man was he:
"Will ye kiss my wife before my een,
And sca'd me wi' pudding bree?"

Then up and started our goodwife,
Gied three skips on the floor:
"Goodman, you've spoken the foremost word;
Get up and bar the door."

The Child Is Father to the Man

'The child is father to the man.'
How can he be? The words are wild.
Suck any sense from that who can:
'The child is father to the man.'
No; what the poet did write ran,
'The man is father to the child.'
'The child is father to the man!'
How *can* he be? The words are wild.

Father William

'You are old, Father William,' the young man said,
'And your hair has become very white;
And yet you incessantly stand on your head—
Do you think, at your age, it is right?'

'In my youth,' Father William replied to his son,
'I feared it might injure the brain;
But, now that I'm perfectly sure I have none,
Why, I do it again and again.'

'You are old,' said the youth, 'as I mentioned before,
And have grown most uncommonly fat;
Yet you turned a back-somersault in at the door—
Pray, what is the reason of that?'

'In my youth,' said the sage, as he shook his grey
locks,
'I kept all my limbs very supple
By the use of this ointment—one shilling the box—
Allow me to sell you a couple?'

'You are old,' said the youth, 'and your jaws are
too weak
For anything tougher than suet;
Yet you finished the goose, with the bones and
the beak—
Pray, how did you manage to do it?'

'In my youth,' said his father, 'I took to the law,
And argued each case with my wife;
And the muscular strength, which it gave to my jaw,
Has lasted the rest of my life.'

'You are old,' said the youth, 'one would hardly suppose
That your eye was as steady as ever;
Yet you balanced an eel on the end of your nose—
What made you so awfully clever?'

'I have answered three questions, and that is enough,'
Said his father; 'don't give yourself airs!
Do you think I can listen all day to such stuff?
Be off, or I'll kick you down stairs!'

"The Clown's Song"

from *TWELFTH NIGHT*

When that I was and a little tiny boy,
  With hey, ho, the wind and the rain,
A foolish thing was but a toy,
  For the rain it raineth every day.

But when I came to man's estate,
  With hey, ho, the wind and the rain,
'Gainst knaves and thieves men shut their gate,
  For the rain it raineth every day.

But when I came, alas! to wive,
  With hey, ho, the wind and the rain,
By swaggering could I never thrive,
  For the rain it raineth every day.

But when I came unto my beds,
  With hey, ho, the wind and the rain,
With toss-pots still had drunken heads,
  For the rain it raineth every day.

A great while ago the world begun,
  With hey, ho, the wind and the rain:—
But that's all one, our play is done,
  And we'll strive to please you every day.

Incidents in the Life of My Uncle Arly

I

O my agèd Uncle Arly!
Sitting on a heap of Barley
    Thro' the silent hours of night,—
Close beside a leafy thicket:—
On his nose there was a Cricket,—
In his hat a Railway-Ticket;—
    (But his shoes were far too tight.)

II

Long ago, in youth, he squander'd
All his goods away, and wander'd
    To the Tiniskoop-hills afar.
There on golden sunsets blazing,
Every evening found him gazing,—
Singing,—'Orb! you're quite amazing!
    How I wonder what you are!'

III

Like the ancient Medes and Persians,
Always by his own exertions
    He subsisted on those hills;—

stanza continues

Whiles, — by teaching children spelling, —
Or at times by merely yelling, —
Or at intervals by selling
    Propter's Nicodemus Pills.

IV

Later, in his morning rambles
He perceived the moving brambles —
    Something square and white disclose; —
'Twas a First-class Railway-Ticket;
But, on stooping down to pick it
Off the ground, — a pea-green Cricket
    Settled on my uncle's Nose.

V

Never — never more, — oh! never,
Did that Cricket leave him ever, —
    Dawn or evening, day or night; —
Clinging as a constant treasure, —
Chirping with a cheerious measure, —
Wholly to my uncle's pleasure, —
    (Though his shoes were far too tight.)

VI

So for three-and-forty winters,
Till his shoes were worn to splinters,
    All those hills he wander'd o'er, —

stanza continues

Sometimes silent;—sometimes yelling;—
Till he came to Borley-Melling,
Near his old ancestral dwelling;—
    (But his shoes were far too tight.)

VII

On a little heap of Barley
Died my agèd uncle Arly,
    And they buried him one night;—
Close behind the leafy thicket;—
There,—his hat and Railway-Ticket;—
There,—his ever-faithful Cricket;—
    (But his shoes were far too tight.)

A Chronicle

Once—but no matter when—
  There lived—no matter where—
A man, whose name—but then
  I need not that declare.

He—well, he had been born,
  And so he was alive;
His age—I details scorn—
  Was somethingty and five.

He lived—how many years
  I truly can't decide;
But this one fact appears
  He lived—until he died.

"He died," I have averred,
  But cannot prove 'twas so,
But that he was interred,
  At any rate, I know.

I fancy he'd a son,
  I hear he had a wife:
Perhaps he'd more than one,
  I know not, on my life!

ANONYMOUS

But whether he was rich,
  Or whether he was poor,
Or neither—both—or which,
  I cannot say, I'm sure.

I can't recall his name,
  Or what he used to do:
But then—well, such is fame!
  'Twill so serve me and you.

And that is why I thus,
  About this unknown man
Would fain create a fuss,
  To rescue, if I can.

From dark oblivion's blow,
  Some record of his lot:
But, ah! I do not know
  Who—where—when—why—or what.

MORAL

In this brief pedigree
  A moral we should find—
But what it ought to be
  Has quite escaped my mind!

A Great Man

Ye muses, pour the pitying tear
  For Pollio snatch'd away:
For had he liv'd another year!
  —He had not dy'd to-day.

O, were he born to bless mankind,
  In virtuous times of yore,
Heroes themselves had fallen behind!
  —Whene'er he went before.

How sad the groves and plains appear,
  And sympathetic sheep:
Even pitying hills would drop a tear!
  —If hills could learn to weep.

His bounty in exalted strain
  Each bard might well display:
Since none implor'd relief in vain!
—That went reliev'd away.

And hark! I hear the tuneful throng;
  His obsequies forbid.
He still shall live, shall live as long
  —As ever dead man did.

There Was a Mad Man

There was a Mad Man,
And he had a Mad Wife,
And they lived in a Mad town,
They had three Children
All at a Birth,
And they were Mad
Every One.

The Father was Mad,
The Mother was Mad,
The Children all Mad besides,
And they all got
Upon a Mad Horse,
And Madly they did ride.

They rode by night and they rode by day,
Yet never a one of them fell,
They rode so madly all the way,
Till they came to the gates of hell.

Old Nick was glad to see them so mad,
And gladly let them in:
But he soon grew sorry to see him so merry,
And let them out again.

The Wise Men of Gotham

In a bowl to sea went wise men three
  On a brilliant night of June:
They carried a net, and their hearts were set
  On fishing up the moon.

The sea was calm, the air was balm,
  Not a breath stirred low or high,
And the moon, I trow, lay as bright below,
  And as round as in the sky.

The wise men with the current went,
  Nor paddle nor oar had they,
And still as the grave they went on the wave,
  That they might not disturb their prey.

Far, far at sea, were the wise men three,
  When their fishing net they threw;
And at their throw, the moon below
  In a thousand fragments flew.

The sea was bright with the dancing light
  Of a million million gleams,
Which the broken moon shot forth as soon
  As the net disturbed her beams.

They drew in their net it was empty and wet:
  And they had lost their pain,
Soon ceased the play of each dancing ray,
  And the image was round again.

Three times they threw, three times they drew,
  And all the while were mute;
And ever anew their wonder grew,
  Till they could not but dispute.

Their silence they broke, and each one spoke
  Full long, and loud, and clear;
A man at sea their voices three
  Full three leagues off might hear.

The three wise men got home again
  To their children and their wives:
But touching their trip, and their net's vain dip,
  They disputed all their lives.

The wise men three could never agree,
  Why they missed the promised boon;
They agreed alone that their net they had thrown,
  And they had not caught the moon. . . .

Three Wise Men of Gotham

Three wise men of Gotham
Went to sea in a bowl;
If the bowl had been stronger,
My song had been longer.

Turvey Top

'Twas after a supper of Norfolk brawn
  That into a doze I chanced to drop,
And thence awoke in the gray of dawn,
  In the wonder-land of Turvey Top.

A land so strange I never had seen,
  And could not choose but look and laugh—
A land where the small the great includes,
  And the whole is less than the half!

A land where the circles were not lines
  Round central points, as schoolmen show,
And the parallels met whenever they chose,
  And went playing at touch-and-go!

There—except that every round was square
  And save that all the squares were rounds—
No surface had limits anywhere,
  So they never could beat the bounds.

In their gardens, fruit before blossom came,
  And the trees diminished as they grew;
And you never went out to walk a mile,
  'Twas the mile that walked to you.

continues

ANONYMOUS

The people there are not tall or short,
  Heavy or light, or stout or thin,
And their lives begin where they should leave off,
  Or leave off where they should begin.

There childhood, with naught of childish glee,
  Looks on the world with thoughtful brow;
'Tis only the aged who laugh and crow,
  And cry, "We have done with it now!"

A singular race! what lives they spent!
  Got up before they went to bed!
And never a man said what he meant,
  Or a woman meant what she said.

They blended colours that will not blend,
  All hideous contrasts voted sweet;
In yellow and red their Quakers dress'd,
  And considered it rather neat.

They didn't believe in the wise and good,
  Said the best were worst, the wisest fools;
And 'twas only to have their teachers taught
  That they founded national schools.

They read in "books that are no books,"
  Their classics—chess-boards neatly bound;
Those their greatest authors who never wrote,
  And their deepest the least profound.

Now, such were the folks of that wonder-land,
  A curious people, as you will own;
But are there none of the race abroad,
  Are no specimens elsewhere known?

Well, I think that he whose views of life
  Are crooked, wrong, perverse, and odd,
Who looks upon all with jaundiced eyes—
  Sees himself and believes it God,

Who sneers at the good, and makes the ill,
  Curses a world he cannot mend;
Who measures life by the rule of wrong
  And abuses its aim and end,

The man who stays when he ought to move,
  And only goes when he ought to stop—
Is strangely like the folk in my dream,
  And would flourish in Turvey Top.

An Elegy on that Glory of Her Sex, Mrs. Mary Blaize

Good people all, with one accord,
  Lament for Madame BLAIZE,
Who never wanted a good word—
  From those who spoke her praise.

The needy seldom passed her door,
  And always found her kind;
She freely lent to all the poor,—
  Who left a pledge behind.

She strove the neighbourhood to please,
  With manners wondrous winning,
And never followed wicked ways,—
  Unless when she was sinning.

At church, in silks and satins new,
  With hoop of monstrous size,
She never slumbered in her pew,—
  But when she shut her eyes.

Her love was sought, I do aver,
  By twenty beaux and more;
The king himself has followed her,—
  When she has walked before.

OLIVER GOLDSMITH (1728–1774)

But now her wealth and finery fled,
  Her hangers-on cut short all;
The doctors found, when she was dead,—
  Her last disorder mortal.

Let us lament, in sorrow sore,
  For Kent-Street well may say,
That had she lived a twelve-month more,—
  She had not died to-day.

Belaġcholly Days

Chilly Dovebber with his boadigg blast
  Dow cubs add strips the bedow add the lawd,
Eved October's suddy days are past—
    Add Subber's gawd!

I kdow dot what it is to which I cligg
  That stirs to sogg add sorrow, yet I trust
That still I sigg, but as the liddets sigg—
    Because I bust.

Add dow, farewell to roses add to birds,
  To larded fields and trigkligg streablets eke;
Farewell to all articulated words
    I faid would speak.

Farewell, by cherished strolliggs od the sward,
  Greed glades and forest shades, farewell to you;
With sorrowigg heart I, wretched add forlord,
    Bid you—achew!!!

Hit or Miss

[Pairs of premisses in search of conclusions]

No bald person needs a hair-brush;
No lizards have hair.

No pins are ambitious;
No needles are pins.

Some oysters are silent;
No silent creatures are amusing.

No frogs write books;
Some people use ink in writing books.

Some mountains are insurmountable;
All stiles can be surmounted.

No lobsters are unreasonable;
No reasonable creatures expect impossibilities.

No fossil can be crossed in love;
An oyster may be crossed in love.

A prudent man shuns hyænas;
No banker is imprudent.

continues

No misers are unselfish;
None but misers save egg-shells.

No military men write poetry;
No generals are civilians.

All owls are satisfactory;
Some excuses are unsatisfactory.

A Copy of Non Sequitors

Great Jack of Lent, clad in a robe of air,
Threw mountains higher than Alcides' beard:
Whilst Pancras Church, arm'd with a sapphire blade,
Began to reason on the business thus:
Ye squand'ring Troglodites of Amsterdam,
How long shall Cerberus a tapster be?
What if stout Ajax lay with Proserpine,
Must men leave eating powder'd beef for that?
For in the Commentaries of Tower Ditch
A fat stew'd bawd hath been a dish of state.
Will you forbid a man to pick his teeth,
Cause Brutus with a sword did slay himself?
Or if an humble bee do kill a whale,
With the butt end of the antarctic pole?
Why these are not the things at which we aim:
More might be said, but then more must be spoke,
The weights fell down because the jackrope broke.
  And he that of these verses maketh doubt,
  Let him sit down and pick the meaning out.

ANONYMOUS

The Amphisbaena or, the Limits of Human Knowledge

Amphisbaena: a serpent supposed to have two heads, and by consequence to move with either end foremost —JOHNSON

If you should happen to descry
An Amphisbaena drawing nigh,
You may remain upon the spot,
But probably had better not.
The prudent its approach avoid
And do not stop to be annoyed,
For all who see it are perplexed
And wonder what will happen next.
Both ends, unfortunately, are
So singularly similar.
It has indeed a head in front
(As has the Indian elephant),
But then, to our alarm, we find
It has another head behind;
And hence zoologists affirm
That it is not a pachyderm.
Until it starts, you never know
In which direction it will go,
Nor can you even then maintain
That it will not come back again.
The sportsman, in amaze profound
Collapsing on his faithful hound,

Exclaims, as soon as he can speak,
'The Amphisbaena is unique.'
Unique no doubt it is; but oh,
That is not what distracts me so.
No: when before my musing eye
The Amphisbaena rambles by,
The question which bereaves of bliss
My finite intellect is this:
Who, who, oh, who will make it clear
Which is the front and which the rear?
Whether, at any given date,
The reptile is advancing straight,
Or whether it is hind-before,
Remains obscure for evermore.
Philosophy, with head of snow,
Confesses that it does not know;
Logicians have debated long,
Which is the right end, which the wrong;
But all their efforts are in vain.
They will not ever ascertain.

The Higher Pantheism in a Nutshell

One, who is not, we see; but one, whom we see
  not, is;
Surely, this is not that; but that is assuredly this.

What, and wherefore, and whence: for under is
  over and under;
If thunder could be without lightning, lightning
  could be without thunder.

Doubt is faith in the main; but faith, on the whole,
  is doubt;
We cannot believe by proof; but could we believe
  without?

Why, and whither, and how? for barley and rye are
  not clover;
Neither are straight lines curves; yet over is under
  and over.

One and two are not one; but one and nothing
  is two;
Truth can hardly be false, if falsehood cannot
  be true.

Parallels all things are; yet many of these are askew;
You are certainly I; but certainly I am not you.

One, whom we see not, is; and one, who is not,
we see;
Fiddle, we know, is diddle; and diddle, we take it,
is dee.

Metaphysics

Why and Wherefore set out one day
  To hunt for a wild Negation.
They agreed to meet at a cool retreat
  On the Point of Interrogation.

But the night was dark and they missed their mark,
  And, driven well-nigh to distraction,
They lost their ways in a murky maze
  Of utter abstruse abstraction.

Then they took a boat and were soon afloat
  On a sea of Speculation,
But the sea grew rough, and their boat, though
    tough,
  Was split into an Equation.

As they floundered about in the waves of doubt
  Rose a fearful Hypothesis,
Who gibbered with glee as they sank in the sea,
  And the last they saw was this:

On a rock-bound reef of Unbelief
  There sat the wild Negation;
Then they sank once more and were washed ashore
  At the Point of Interrogation.

 OLIVER HERFORD (1863–1935)

The Table and the Chair

Said the Table to the Chair,
"You can hardly be aware
How I suffer from the heat
And from chilblains on my feet.
If we took a little walk,
We might have a little talk.
Pray let us take the air,"
Said the Table to the Chair.

Said the Chair unto the Table,
"Now, you *know* we are not able;
How foolishly you talk,
When you know we *cannot* walk!"
Said the Table with a sigh,
"It can do no harm to try.
I've as many legs as you;
Why can't we walk on two?"

So they both went slowly down,
And walked about the town
With a cheerful bumpy sound
As they toddled round and round;
And everybody cried,
As they hastened to their side,

stanza continues

EDWARD LEAR (1812–1888)

"See! The Table and the Chair
Have come out to take the air!"

But in going down an alley
To a castle in a valley,
They completely lost their way,
And wandered all the day;
Till, to see them safely back,
They paid a Ducky-Quack,
And a Beetle, and a Mouse,
Who took them to their house.

Then they whispered to each other,
"O delightful little brother,
What a lovely walk we've taken!
Let us dine on beans and bacon."
So the Ducky and the leetle
Browny-Mousy and the Beetle
Dined, and danced upon their heads
Till they toddled to their beds.

Falling Up

I tripped on my shoelace
And I fell up—
Up to the roof tops,
Up over the town,
Up past the tree tops,
Up over the mountains,
Up where the colors
Blend into the sounds.
But it got me so dizzy
When I looked around,
I got sick to my stomach
And I threw down.

The State of Shrovetide

'Tis a wonderful thing, continued Xenomanes, to hear and see the state of Shrovetide.

If he chanced to spit, it was whole basketsful of goldfinches.
If he blowed his nose, it was pickled grigs.
When he wept, it was ducks with onion sauce.
When he sneezed, it was whole tubfuls of mustard.
When he coughed, it was boxes of marmalade.
When he sobbed, it was watercresses.
When he yawned, it was potfuls of pickled peas.
When he sighed, it was dried neats' tongues.
When he whistled, it was a whole scuttleful of green apes.
When he snored, it was a whole panful of fried beans.
When he frowned, it was soused hogs' feet.
When he spoke, it was coarse brown russet cloth; so little it was like crimson silk, with which Parisatis desired that the words of such as spoke to her son Cyrus, King of Persia, should be interwoven.
When he blowed, it was indulgence money-boxes.
When he winked, it was buttered buns.
When he grumbled, it was March cats.
When he nodded, it was ironbound waggons.
When he made mouths, it was broken staves.

When he trembled, it was large venison pasties.
When he did sweat, it was old ling with butter sauce.
When he belched, it was bushels of oysters.
When he muttered, it was lawyers' revels.
When he hopped about, it was letters of licence and protections.
When he stepped back, it was sea cockle-shells.
When he slabbered, it was common ovens.
When he was hoarse, it was an entry of morrice-dancers.
When he broke wind, it was dun cows' leather spatterdashes.
When he funked, it was washed-leather boots.
When he scratched himself, it was new proclamations.
When he sung, it was peas in cods.
When he evacuated, it was mushrooms and morilles.
When he puffed, it was cabbages with oil, alias caules amb'olif.
When he talked, it was the last year's snow.
When he dreamt, it was of a cock and a bull.
When he gave nothing, so much for the bearer.
If he thought to himself, it was whimsies and maggots.
If he dozed, it was leases of lands.

Translated from the French by
Sir Thomas Urquhart (1611–1660)

The Palace of Humbug

I dreamt I dwelt in marble halls,
And each damp thing that creeps and crawls
Went wobble-wobble on the walls.

Faint odours of departed cheese,
Blown on the dank, unwholesome breeze,
Awoke the never-ending sneeze.

Strange pictures decked the arras drear,
Strange characters of woe and fear,
The humbugs of the social sphere.

One showed a vain and noisy prig,
That shouted empty words and big
At him that nodded in a wig.

And one, a dotard grim and gray,
Who wasteth childhood's happy day
In work more profitless than play.

Whose icy breast no pity warms,
Whose little victims sit in swarms,
And slowly sob on lower forms.

LEWIS CARROLL (1832–1898)

And one, a green thyme-honoured Bank,
Where flowers are growing wild and rank,
Like weeds that fringe a poisoned tank.

All birds of evil omen there
Flood with rich Notes the tainted air,
The witless wanderer to snare.

The fatal Notes neglected fall,
No creature heeds the treacherous call,
For all those goodly Strawn Baits pall.

The wandering phantom broke and fled,
Straightway I saw within my head
A vision of a ghostly bed,

Where lay two worn decrepit men,
The fictions of a lawyer's pen,
Who never more might breathe again.

The serving-man of Richard Roe
Wept, inarticulate with woe:
She wept, that waited on John Doe.

'Oh rouse,' I urged, 'the waning sense
With tales of tangled evidence,
Of suit, demurrer, and defence.'

continues

'Vain,' she replied, 'such mockeries:
For morbid fancies, such as these,
No suits can suit, no plea can please.'

And bending o'er that man of straw,
She cried in grief and sudden awe,
Not inappropriately, 'Law!'

The well-remembered voice he knew,
He smiled, he faintly muttered 'Sue!'
(Her very name was legal too.)

The night was fled, the dawn was nigh:
A hurricane went raving by,
And swept the Vision from mine eye.

Vanished that dim and ghostly bed,
(The hangings, tape; the tape was red:)
'Tis o'er, and Doe and Roe are dead!

Oh, yet my spirit inly crawls,
What time it shudderingly recalls
That horrid dream of marble halls!

"If all the world were paper,"

If all the world were paper,
And all the sea were ink,
If all the trees were bread and cheese,
How should we do for drink?

If all the world were sand O,
Oh then what should we lack O,
If as they say there were no clay,
How should we take tobacco?

If all our vessels ran-a,
If none but had a crack-a,
If Spanish apes ate all the grapes,
How should we do for sack-a?

If all the world were men,
And men lived all in trenches,
And there were none but we alone,
How should we do for wenches?

If friars had no bald pates,
Nor nuns had no dark cloisters,
If all the seas were beans and peas,
How should we do for oysters?

continues

If there had been no projects,
  Nor none that did great wrongs,
If fiddlers shall turn players all,
  How should we do for songs?

If all things were eternal,
  And nothing their end bringing,
If this should be, then how should we
  Here make an end of singing?

Russian and Turk

There was a Russian came over the sea,
Just when the war was growing hot;
And his name it was Tjalikavakaree-
Karindobrolikanahudarot-
Shibkadirova-
Ivarditztova
Sanilik
Danerik
Varagobhot.

A Turk was standing upon the shore—
Right where the terrible Russian crossed,
And he cried: "Bismillah! I'm Ab-El Kor-
Bazarou-Kilgonautosgobross-
Getfinpravadi-
Kligekoladji
Grivino
Blivido-
Jenikodosk!

So they stood like brave men long and well;
And they called each other their proper names,
Till the lockjaw seized them, and where they fell

stanza continues

They buried them both by the Irdesholmmes
Kalatalustchuk
Mischtaribusiclup-
Bulgari-
Dulbary-
Sagharimsing.

"One old Oxford ox opening oysters;"

One old Oxford ox opening oysters;
Two tee-totums totally tired of trying to trot
  to Tadbury;
Three tall tigers tippling tenpenny tea;
Four fat friars fanning fainting flies;
Five frippy Frenchmen foolishly fishing for flies;
Six sportsmen shooting snipes;
Seven Severn salmons swallowing shrimps;
Eight Englishmen eagerly examining Europe;
Nine nimble noblemen nibbling nonpareils;
Ten tinkers tinkling upon ten tin tinder-boxes with
  ten tenpenny tacks;
Eleven elephants elegantly equipt;
Twelve typographical topographers typically
  translating types.

A Fancy

When Piecrust first began to reign,
  Cheese-parings went to war,
Red Herrings lookt both blue and wan,
  Green Leeks and Puddings jar.
Blind Hugh went out to see
  Two cripples run a race,
The Ox fought with the Humble Bee
  And claw'd him by the face.

"Ariel's Song"

from *THE TEMPEST*

Where the bee sucks, there suck I:
In a cowslip's bell I lie;
There I couch when owls do cry.
On the bat's back I do fly
After summer merrily.
Merrily, merrily shall I live now
Under the blossom that hangs on the bough.

The Man in the Wilderness

The man in the wilderness asked of me,
How many strawberries grew in the sea?
I answered him as I thought good
As many red herrings as grew in a wood.

We're All in the Dumps

We're all in the dumps,
For diamonds are trumps,
The kittens are gone to St. Paul's,
The babies are bit,
The moon's in a fit
And the houses are built without walls.

The Red Herring

Herring and ling!
  O herring and ling!
Of all the fish in the sea
  Is Herring the king.

Oh, what do you think
  I made of his head?
I made as fine oven
  As ever baked bread.
Herring and ling, O herring and ling,
Don't you think I did well with my red herring?

Oh, what do you think
  I made of his fins?
I made a whole parcel
  Of needles and pins.
Herring and ling, O herring and ling,
Don't you think I did well with my red herring?

Oh, what do you think
  I made of his eyes?
I made a whole parcel
  Of puddings and pies.
Herring and ling, O herring and ling,
Don't you think I did well with my red herring?

ANONYMOUS

Oh, what do you think
  I made of his back?
I made as fine whip
  As you ever did crack.
Herring and ling, O herring and ling,
Don't you think I did well with my red herring?

Oh, what do you think
  I made of his ribs?
I made fifty ox-stalls
  And fifty ox-cribs.
Herring and ling, O herring and ling,
Don't you think I did well with my red herring?

Oh, what do you think
  I made of his breast?
I made fifty good oxen
  As ever yoke pressed.
Herring and ling, O herring and ling.
Don't you think I did well with my red herring?

Oh, what do you think
  I made of his tail?
I made the best ship
  That ever set sail.
Herring and ling, O herring and ling.
Don't you think I did well with my red herring?

Cold Are the Crabs

Cold are the crabs that crawl on yonder hills,
Colder the cucumbers that grow beneath,
And colder still the brazen chops that wreathe
  The tedious gloom of philosophic pills!
For when the tardy film of nectar fills
The ample bowls of demons and of men,
There lurks the feeble mouse, the homely hen,
  And there the porcupine with all her quills.
Yet much remains—to weave a solemn strain
That lingering sadly—slowly dies away,
Daily departing with departing day
A pea green gamut on a distant plain
When wily walrusses in congress meet—
  Such such is life—

The Silver Question

The Sun appeared so smug and bright,
  One day, that I made bold
To ask him what he did each night
  With all his surplus gold.

He flushed uncomfortably red,
  And would not meet my eye.
"I travel round the world," he said,
  "And travelling rates are high."

With frigid glance I pierced him through.
  He squirmed and changed his tune.
Said he: "I will be frank with you:
  I lend it to the Moon.

"Poor thing! You know she's growing old
  And hasn't any folk.
She suffers terribly from cold,
  And half the time she's broke."

. . . .

That evening on the beach I lay
  Behind a lonely dune,
And as she rose above the bay
  I buttonholed the Moon.

continues

OLIVER HERFORD (1863–1935)

"Tell me about that gold," said I.
  I saw her features fall.
"You see, it's useless to deny;
  The Sun has told me all."

"Sir!" she exclaimed, "how *can* you try
  An honest Moon this way?
As for the gold, I put it by
  Against a rainy day."

I smiled and shook my head. "All right,
  If you *must* know," said she,
"I change it into silver bright
  Wherewith to tip the Sea.

"He is so faithful and so good,
  A most deserving case;
If he should leave, I fear it would
  Be hard to fill his place."

• • • • • • • •

When asked if they accepted tips,
  The waves became so rough;
I thought of those at sea in ships,
  And felt I'd said enough.

For if one virtue I have learned,
  'Tis *tact*; so I forbore
To press the matter, though I burned
  To ask one question more.

I hate a scene, and do not wish
  To be mixed up in gales,
But, oh, I longed to ask the Fish
  Whence came their silver scales!

The Walrus and the Carpenter

The sun was shining on the sea,
  Shining with all his might:
He did his very best to make
  The billows smooth and bright—
And this was odd, because it was
  The middle of the night.

The moon was shining sulkily,
  Because she thought the sun
Had got no business to be there
  After the day was done—
'It's very rude of him,' she said,
  'To come and spoil the fun!'

The sea was wet as wet could be,
  The sands were dry as dry.
You could not see a cloud, because
  No cloud was in the sky:
No birds were flying overhead—
  There were no birds to fly.

The Walrus and the Carpenter
  Were walking close at hand;
They wept like anything to see

stanza continues

Such quantities of sand:
'If this were only cleared away,'
They said, 'it *would* be grand!'

'If seven maids with seven mops
Swept it for half a year,
Do you suppose,' the Walrus said,
'That they could get it clear?'
'I doubt it,' said the Carpenter,
And shed a bitter tear.

'O Oysters, come and walk with us!'
The Walrus did beseech.
'A pleasant walk, a pleasant talk,
Along the briny beach:
We cannot do with more than four,
To give a hand to each.'

The eldest Oyster looked at him,
But never a word he said:
The eldest Oyster winked his eye,
And shook his heavy head—
Meaning to say he did not choose
To leave the oyster-bed.

But four young Oysters hurried up,
All eager for the treat:

stanza continues

Their coats were brushed, their faces washed,
  Their shoes were clean and neat—
And this was odd, because, you know,
  They hadn't any feet.

Four other Oysters followed them,
  And yet another four;
And thick and fast they came at last,
  And more, and more, and more—
All hopping through the frothy waves,
  And scrambling to the shore.

The Walrus and the Carpenter
  Walked on a mile or so,
And then they rested on a rock
  Conveniently low:
And all the little Oysters stood
  And waited in a row.

'The time has come,' the Walrus said,
  'To talk of many things:
Of shoes—and ships—and sealing-wax—
  Of cabbages—and kings—
And why the sea is boiling hot—
  And whether pigs have wings.'

'But wait a bit,' the Oysters cried,
  'Before we have our chat;

For some of us are out of breath,
  And all of us are fat!'
'No hurry!' said the Carpenter.
  They thanked him much for that.

'A loaf of bread,' the Walrus said,
  'Is what we chiefly need:
Pepper and vinegar besides
  Are very good indeed—
Now if you're ready, Oysters dear,
  We can begin to feed.'

'But not on us!' the Oysters cried,
  Turning a little blue.
'After such kindness, that would be
  A dismal thing to do!'
'The night is fine,' the Walrus said.
  'Do you admire the view?'

'It was so kind of you to come!
  And you are very nice!'
The Carpenter said nothing but
  'Cut us another slice:
I wish you were not quite so deaf—
  I've had to ask you twice!'

continues

'It seems a shame,' the Walrus said.
'To play them such a trick,
After we've brought them out so far,
And made them trot so quick!'
The Carpenter said nothing but
'The butter's spread too thick!'

'I weep for you,' the Walrus said:
'I deeply sympathize.'
With sobs and tears he sorted out
Those of the largest size,
Holding his pocket-handkerchief
Before his streaming eyes.

'O Oysters,' said the Carpenter,
'You've had a pleasant run!
Shall we be trotting home again?'
But answer came there none —
And this was scarcely odd, because
They'd eaten every one.

A Sailor's Yarn

This is the tale that was told to me,
By a battered and shattered son of the sea:
To me and my messmate, Silas Green,
When I was a guileless young marine.

"'Twas the good ship 'Gyacutus,'
All in the China seas;
With the wind a lee, and the capstan free,
To catch the summer breeze.

"'Twas Captain Porgie on the deck
To the mate in the mizzen hatch,
While the boatswain bold, in the for'ard hold,
Was winding his larboard watch.

"'Oh, how does our good ship head to-night?
How heads our gallant craft?'
'Oh, she heads to the E. S. W. by N.
And the binnacle lies abaft.'

"'Oh, what does the quadrant indicate?
And how does the sextant stand?'
'Oh, the sextant's down to the freezing point
And the quadrant's lost a hand.'

continues

"'Oh, if the quadrant's lost a hand,
And the sextant falls so low,
It's our body and bones to Davy Jones
This night are bound to go.'

"'Oh, fly aloft to the garboard-strake,
And reef the spanker boom,
Bend a stubbing sail on the martingale
To give her weather room.'

" 'Oh, boatswain, down in the for'ard hold
What water do you find?'
'Four foot and a half by the royal gaff
And rather more behind.'

"'Oh, sailors, collar your marline spikes
And each belaying pin;
Come, stir your stumps to spike the pumps,
Or more will be coming in.'

" 'They stirred their stumps, they spiked the pumps
They spliced the mizzen brace;
Aloft and alow they worked, but, oh!
The water gained apace.'

"They bored a hole below her line
To let the water out,
But more and more with awful roar
The water in did spout.

"Then up spoke the cook of our gallant ship—
And he was a lubber brave—
'I've several wives in various ports,
And my life I'd like to save.'

"Then up spoke the captain of marines,
Who dearly loved his prog:
'It's awful to die, and it's worse to be dry,
And I move we pipes to grog.'

"Oh, then 'twas the gallant second-mate
As stopped them sailors' jaw,
'Twas the second-mate whose hand had weight
In laying down the law.

"He took the anchor on his back,
And leapt into the main;
Through foam and spray he clove his way,
And sunk, and rose again.

"Through foam and spray a league away
The anchor stout he bore,
Till, safe at last, I made it fast,
And warped the ship ashore."

This is the tale that was told to me,
By that modest and truthful son of the sea.

stanza continues

And I envy the life of a second mate,
Though captains curse him and sailors hate;
For he ain't like some of the swabs I've seen,
As would go and lie to a poor marine.

O'er Seas That Have No Beaches

O'er seas that have no beaches
To end their waves upon,
I floated with twelve peaches,
A sofa and a swan.

The blunt waves crashed above us
The sharp waves burst around,
There was no one to love us,
No hope of being found—

Where, on the notched horizon
So endlessly a-drip,
I saw all of a sudden
No sign of any ship.

The Jumblies

I

They went to sea in a Sieve, they did,
  In a Sieve they went to sea:
In spite of all their friends could say,
On a winter's morn, on a stormy day,
  In a Sieve they went to sea!
And when the Sieve turned round and round,
And every one cried, 'You'll all be drowned!'
They called aloud, 'Our Sieve ain't big,
But we don't care a button! we don't care a fig!
  In a Sieve we'll go to sea!'
    Far and few, far and few,
      Are the lands where the Jumblies live;
    Their heads are green, and their hands are blue,
      And they went to sea in a Sieve.

II

They sailed in a Sieve, they did,
  In a Sieve they sailed so fast,
With only a beautiful pea-green veil
Tied with a riband by way of a sail,
  To a small tobacco-pipe mast;
And every one said, who saw them go,
'O won't they be soon upset, you know!

stanza continues

For the sky is dark, and the voyage is long,
And happen what may, it's extremely wrong
In a Sieve to sail so fast!'
  Far and few, far and few,
    Are the lands where the Jumblies live;
  Their heads are green, and their hands are blue,
    And they went to sea in a Sieve.

III

The water it soon came in, it did,
  The water it soon came in;
So to keep them dry, they wrapped their feet
In a pinky paper all folded neat,
  And they fastened it down with a pin.
And they passed the night in a crockery-jar,
And each of them said, 'How wise we are!
Though the sky be dark, and the voyage be long,
Yet we never can think we were rash or wrong,
  While round in our Sieve we spin!'
    Far and few, far and few,
      Are the lands where the Jumblies live;
    Their heads are green, and their hands are blue,
      And they went to sea in a Sieve.

IV

And all night long they sailed away;
  And when the sun went down,

stanza continues

They whistled and warbled a moony song
To the echoing sound of a coppery gong,
In the shade of the mountains brown.
'O Timballo! How happy we are,
When we live in a sieve and a crockery-jar,
And all night long in the moonlight pale,
We sail away with a pea-green sail,
In the shade of the mountains brown!'
Far and few, far and few,
Are the lands where the Jumblies live;
Their heads are green, and their hands are blue,
And they went to sea in a Sieve.

V

They sailed to the Western Sea, they did,
To a land all covered with trees,
And they bought an Owl, and a useful Cart,
And a pound of Rice, and a Cranberry Tart,
And a hive of silvery Bees.
And they bought a Pig, and some green Jack-daws,
And a lovely Monkey with lollipop paws,
And forty bottles of Ring-Bo-Ree,
And no end of Stilton Cheese.
Far and few, far and few,
Are the lands where the Jumblies live;
Their heads are green, and their hands are blue,
And they went to sea in a Sieve.

VI

And in twenty years they all came back,
  In twenty years or more,
And every one said, 'How tall they've grown!
For they've been to the Lakes, and the Torrible Zone,
  And the hills of the Chankly Bore';
And they drank their health, and gave them a feast
Of dumplings made of beautiful yeast;
And every one said, 'If we only live,
We too will go to sea in a Sieve,—
  To the hills of the Chankly Bore!'
    Far and few, far and few,
      Are the lands where the Jumblies live;
    Their heads are green, and their hands are blue,
      And they went to sea in a Sieve.

One Fine Day in the Middle of the Night

One fine day in the middle of the night,
Two dead men got up to fight,
Back to back they faced each other,
Drew their swords and shot each other.
A paralysed donkey passing by
Kicked a blind man in the eye,
Knocked him through a nine-inch wall
Into a dry ditch and drowned them all.

The Lugubrious Whing-Whang

Out on the margin of moonshine land,
  Tickle me, love, in these lonesome ribs,
Out where the whing-whang loves to stand,
Writing his name with his tail on the sand,
And wiping it out with his oogerish hand;
  Tickle me, love, in these lonesome ribs.

Is it the gibber of gungs and keeks?
  Tickle me, love, in these lonesome ribs,
Or what *is* the sound the whing-whang seeks,
Crouching low by the winding creeks,
And holding his breath for weeks and weeks?
  Tickle me, love, in these lonesome ribs.

Aroint him the wraithest of wraithly things!
  Tickle me, love, in these lonesome ribs,
'Tis a fair whing-whangess with phosphor rings,
And bridal jewels of fangs and stings,
And she sits and as sadly and softly sings
As the mildewed whir of her own dead wings;
  Tickle me, dear; tickle me here;
  Tickle me, love, in these lonesome ribs.

JAMES WHITCOMB RILEY (1849–1916)

The Dinkey-Bird

In an ocean, 'way out yonder
  (As all sapient people know),
Is the land of Wonder-Wander,
  Whither children love to go;
It's their playing, romping, swinging,
  That give great joy to me
While the Dinkey-Bird goes singing
  In the Amfalula-tree!

There the gum-drops grow like cherries,
  And taffy's thick as peas,—
Caramels you pick like berries
  When, and where, and how you please:
Big red sugar-plums are clinging
  To the cliffs beside that sea
Where the Dinkey-Bird is singing
  In the Amfalula-tree.

So when the children shout and scamper
  And make merry all the day,
When there's naught to put a damper
  To the ardor of their play;
When I hear their laughter ringing,
  Then I'm sure as sure can be

stanza continues

That the Dinkey-Bird is singing
  In the Amfalula-tree.

For the Dinkey-Bird's bravuras
  And staccatos are so sweet—
His roulades, appogiaturas,
  And robustos so complete,
That the youth of every nation—
  Be they near or far away—
Have especial delectation
  In that gladsome roundelay.

Their eyes grow bright and brighter,
  Their lungs begin to crow,
Their hearts get light and lighter,
  And their cheeks are all aglow;
For an echo cometh bringing
  The news to all and me.
That the Dinkey-Bird is singing
  In the Amfalula-tree.

I'm sure you'd like to go there
  To see your feathered friend—
And so many goodies grow there
  You would like to comprehend!

stanza continues

Speed, little dreams, your winging
To that land across the sea
Where the Dinkey-Bird is singing
In the Amfalula-Tree!

The Nutcrackers and the Sugar-tongs

I

The Nutcrackers sate by a plate on the table,
The Sugar-tongs sate by a plate at his side;
And the Nutcrackers said, 'Don't you wish we
were able
'Along the blue hills and green meadows to ride?
'Must we drag on this stupid existence for ever,
'So idle and weary, so full of remorse, —
'While every one else takes his pleasure, and never
'Seems happy unless he is riding a horse?

II

'Don't you think we could ride without being
instructed?
'Without any saddle, or bridle, or spur?
'Our legs are so long, and so aptly constructed,
'I'm sure that an accident could not occur.
'Let us all of a sudden hop down from the table,
'And hustle downstairs, and each jump on a
horse!
'Shall we try? Shall we go? Do you think we are
able?'
The Sugar-tongs answered distinctly, 'Of course!'

continues

III

So down the long staircase they hopped in a
minute,
The Sugar-tongs snapped, and the Crackers said
'crack!'
The stable was open, the horses were in it;
Each took out a pony, and jumped on his back.
The Cat in a fright scrambled out of the doorway,
The Mice tumbled out of a bundle of hay,
The brown and white Rats, and the black ones
from Norway,
Screamed out, 'They are taking the horses away!'

IV

The whole of the household was filled with
amazement,
The Cups and the Saucers danced madly about,
The Plates and the Dishes looked out of the
casement,
The Saltcellar stood on his head with a shout,
The Spoons with a clatter looked out of the lattice,
The Mustard-pot climbed up the Gooseberry
Pies,
The Soup-ladle peeped through a heap of Veal
Patties,
And squeaked with a ladle-like scream of
surprise.

V

The Frying-pan said, 'It's an awful delusion!'
The Tea-kettle hissed and grew black in the face;
And they all rushed downstairs in the wildest
confusion,
To see the great Nutcracker–Sugar-tong race.
And out of the stable, with screamings and
laughter,
(Their ponies were cream-coloured, speckled
with brown,)
The Nutcrackers first, and the Sugar-tongs after,
Rode all round the yard, and then all round the
town.

VI

They rode through the street, and they rode by the
station,
They galloped away to the beautiful shore;
In silence they rode, and 'made no observation',
Save this: 'We will never go back any more!'
And still you might hear, till they rode out of
hearing,
The Sugar-tongs snap, and the Crackers say
'crack!'
Till far in the distance their forms disappearing,
They faded away—and they never came back!

Index of Authors

Index of First Lines

Acknowledgments

"flotsam and jetsam," by E. E. Cummings. Copyright © 1939, © 1967, 1991 by the Trustees for the E. E. Cummings Trust, from COMPLETE POEMS: 1904–1962 by E. E. Cummings, edited by George J. Firmage. Used by permission of Liveright Publishing Corporation.

"Don't Dress Your Cat in an Apron," by Dan Greenburg. Copyright © 1972 by Free To Be Foundation, Inc. Reprinted by permission of Free To Be Foundation, Inc.

"Lydia, The Tattooed Lady," by E. Y. Harburg and Harold Arlen. Copyright © 1939 (Renewed) EMI Feist Catalog Inc. All rights reserved. Used by permission WARNER BROS. PUBLICATIONS U.S. INC., Miami, FL 33014.

"The Parrot," by Christian Morgenstern, translated by Stuart Miller. Translation copyright © 2002 by Stuart Miller.

"The Picket Fence," by Christian Morgenstern, translated by Stuart Miller. Translation copyright © 2002 by Stuart Miller.

"How Pleasant to Ape Mr. Lear," by Ogden Nash. Copyright © 1968 by Ogden Nash. Reprinted by permission of Curtis Brown, Ltd.

"The Private Dining Room," by Ogden Nash. Copyright © 1953 by Ogden Nash. Reprinted by permission of Curtis Brown, Ltd.

"Wendigo," by Ogden Nash. Copyright © 1953 by Ogden Nash. Reprinted by permission of Curtis Brown, Ltd.